The Learning Advantage

Blending Technology, Strategy, and Learning to Create Lasting Results

Karen Mantyla and Contributors

Michael Gerwitz
Fred Goh
Michael Hatt
Michael Malehorn
Susan Meisinger
Craig Mindrum
Kurt Olson
Don Vanthournout

ASTD
PRESS

Alexandria, Virginia

ASTD Press is an internationally renowned source of insightful and practical information on workplace learning and performance topics, including training basics, evaluation and return-on-investment, instructional systems development, e-learning, leadership, and career development.

Ordering information: Books published by ASTD Press can be purchased by visiting our website at store.astd.org or by calling 800.628.2783 or 703.683.8100.

Library of Congress Control Number: 2007931356

ISBN-13: 978-1-56286-503-0

ASTD Press Editorial Staff:

Director: Dean Smith
Manager, Acquisitions and Author Relations: Mark Morrow
Editorial Manager: Jacqueline Edlund-Braun
Senior Associate Editor: Tora Estep
Editorial Assistant: Gina Del Priore

Copyeditor: Scott Long
Indexer: April Davis
Proofreader: Kris Patenaude
Typography Design and Composition: Kathleen Schaner
Cover Design: Katherine Warminsky
Cover Illustration: Getty Images

Printed by Versa Press Inc., East Peoria, IL, www.versapress.com

To

Christopher

The future is in your technology-supported hands

■ ■ ■ ■ Contents

In my 15 years at QUALCOMM, I have never been asked to cut the learning budget. It's really important for all organizations to remember that people are the largest asset that they have. Development of people and making an investment in people even during tough times is critically important. We want to make sure that we attract great talent, we retain that talent, and we develop that talent. When times are tough, having people leave the organization is not something that organizations want to go through. We believe it's really important to actually increase the investment that you have in employee development during times that are tough because that's going to help your investment later on as a business and help your business grow.

—Tamar Elkeles

Vice President, Learning and Organization Development

QUALCOMM

■ ■ ■

One of the most stressful and frustrating moments in my more-than-25-year professional career was the moment I learned that my training budget was to be cut for "budgetary reasons." Has this happened to you? Given the critical role that workplace learning plays in the ultimate success of a company, I am sure you recognize the source of my frustration. At a time when maximizing the performance of the organizations' greatest assets (employees) is so important, many organizations still follow the same budget-slashing pattern.

In my professional career as a training specialist, I've seen lots of training budgets cut by senior executives when the enterprise needed a budget adjustment. I bet if you did a random sampling of training professionals and asked, "What area is most likely to be cut when the budget shears are open wide?" they would say, "Training." I wonder how many readers are thinking the same thing.

Why does this knee-jerk reaction happen so easily when decisions are made at the executive level? Sadly, the reason is simple—many at the C level still believe training, learning, self-improvement, or any other term you choose to use is nonessential to the enterprise and, as such, is expendable.

The companies and organizations featured in this book are the exceptions to the rule. They have discovered the value of keeping training budgets aligned to strategy intact and ultimately make a good case for keeping them that way.

My role is to be the facilitator for these case studies. The goal for readers is to determine how they can apply these documented success stories to their own situations and organizations. If you can find one or more ideas that will help you keep training dollars in your budget, that's your return-on-investment (ROI) for the book.

In each case presented here, you will see that the use of technology plays an important part in delivering the content as well as in the overall strategy of the enterprise. Technology might include creative use of the Internet or a website or the use of a learning management system to help create content to develop a workforce. An infinite variety of ways exist to use technology as the backbone to accomplish strategic goals and justify maintaining stable training funding levels.

Signs of Changing Times

In late January 2007, several political candidates running for U.S. president started a series of webcasts to have a conversation with the citizens of the United States. Not only were the webcasts powerful, they implemented easy-to-use, web-based, blended learning concepts. These webcasts were part of each candidate's overall strategic plan to get elected. The Internet played an important part of every candidate's strategy. They each had their own web presence and YouTube site. In addition, some of them actually used Second Life and had avatars running around talking about their candidacy and issues. Technology was used as a powerful distribution tool to reach the people who make things happen and to engage people in the political process. And it worked.

With the power of technology, coupled with an integrated approach to creating a strategic plan, I can't imagine that these webcasts or web communications would ever have been cut to save funds. Here was a way to provide an important learner (citizen)-centered approach to gaining knowledge about the issues at stake. I learned things I didn't know and probably would not have learned had it not been for the use of Internet-based segments. Webcasts appealed to many different learning styles, including my own. I'm a visual learner; therefore, the video/audio format worked well for me. For those who prefer to read, there were references to websites for further information and updates. The candidates all developed websites, blogs, and used the Internet as a key part of communication for their strategic plan. They also had a debate with YouTube video entries—a first in a campaign process. Now, a new president of the United States has been elected who, in various ways, used technology as a critical part of his run for the White House.

This is a pure example of how creating a blended learning approach into a strategic plan can be viewed as an essential investment directly tied to the bottom line. In addition to webcasts, blogs, and interactivity (ability to ask questions), this blended learning approach includes research information, on-site opportunities, and more.

No Buzz Words

No buzz words will appear in this book. No cute phrases or "tricks of the trade" will be offered as a "how to" to get the dollars you need for your workforce training and development bottom line. There will be no "words du jour" because I want this to be a solid guideline on how to increase your chances of not only saving your training budget, but also creating an executive mindset that sees the strategic value of investing in learning and development. When those in the C suite view learning as a strategic tool to achieve targeted enterprise goals, the training budget is viewed from a different angle—that learning provides documented value to achieving strategic goals.

Correcting the Nonessential Label: Making the Case for the Value of Learning

This book should be used as a guide to thinking about and then reassessing how to position learning as a value-add in your organization—in other words, how to position training as a key factor in achieving the strategic goals of your organization. I have assembled learning advantage case studies of three of the most respected companies in the world—Accenture, Microsoft, and Caterpillar. By reading about their experiences, supplemented with the sophisticated online technology example from Microsoft, you will find lessons and inspiration to build respect for the learning advantage in your own organization. More important, you will see how to integrate and align learning with the strategic plan of your organization. In addition, I provide insightful stories from the U.S. Department of Labor and from an experienced and respected learning consultant. The case studies serve as powerful examples of savvy training strategy and implementation that are firmly connected to their organizations' bottom lines.

Throughout the book, I contribute complementary chapters that provide the context and conceptual frame to understanding the blended learning approach. In chapter 1, I begin with a frank discussion of the real value of learning. In chapter 3, I set the stage for blending technology, learning, and strategy. I make the case for learning and strategic alignment in chapter 7. Finally, in chapter 10 I point the way forward for how you can create ongoing value for your organization. And interspersed between are the success stories from organizations that have made these concepts and ideas work.

Accenture

Accenture is a global management consulting, technology services, and outsourcing company with more than 150,000 employees in 49 countries. Accenture collaborates with both private and public/governmental agencies to build high-performing organizations. In chapter 2, Don Vanthournout and Kurt Olson, Accenture's chief learning officer and director of capability solutions, respectively, describe how their organization fulfills its commitments to external clients and how these same tools have transformed learning at Accenture.

Microsoft

Michael Hatt, former global training manager at Microsoft Corporation, offers an account of his role in the launch of the Xbox and how he got a global sales and customer service workforce ready for the challenge. Hatt's breathtaking 10-week challenge is described in chapter 4, which effectively shows the nexus of strategy, application, and ROI. You will see how ROI for the learning effort was tracked to the penny. Follow along online with the 3-D model simulation of Xbox training used to accomplish this impressive feat (www.astd.org/LearningAdvantage).

U.S. Department of Labor

In chapter 5, Michael Gerwitz, e-learning project manager for the U.S. Department of Labor, and Michael Malehorn, senior manager for e-learning infrastructure at SI International, provide a unique perspective on the challenges of implementing a learning management system in the federal government. In their chapter, "Laboring Over Technology: Taking Steps to Select the Right Blend," you will find a frank discussion about this effort and learn valuable lessons about identifying enterprise needs, building a user workforce, working with contractors, and connecting the learning management system (LMS) to organizational strategy. More important, you will see how technology is blended with other traditional learning for maximum benefit.

Caterpillar University

Caterpillar University is an award-winning, world-class learning institution. Fred Goh, former director of strategic learning at Caterpillar University, shares his valuable insight in chapter 6 on "Managing Learning to Ensure Strategic Alignment with the Business." Goh illustrates how he and his team built a successful program that targets over 94,000 employees around the world. You will learn about the bottom-line savings to the enterprise and how Caterpillar University aligned strategy, technology, and employee development to build its stellar program.

Bonuses in This Book

In addition to these great case studies, I have included a chapter by Craig Mindrum, a professional consultant and educator who shares his clear perspective on why paying attention to learning styles of learners connects both to successful organizational strategy and learning with impact (chapter 8).

The other powerful bonus in this book is a contribution by Susan Meisinger, former president and chief executive officer of SHRM (Society for Human Resource Management). In chapter 9, Meisinger offers her perspective on how learning is tied directly to getting the most out of human capital and how technology will play a key role in transforming organizational performance. She provides a look into the combined future of HR and learning.

Acknowledgment

I want to thank Mark Morrow at ASTD for providing an opportunity to share our knowledge with you. He gave me creative license to design a book from the inside out to facilitate the content and contributions offered here. He is a supportive editor and a driving force for making this book the best it can be.

We are grateful to Patrick Vartuli and C2 Technologies, Inc. for hosting the online 3-D model simulation of the Microsoft Xbox training and for making this value add possible.

The bottom line of this book is to help you create and participate in a learning strategy, so that when the budget knife is out and ready to slice dollars, your program won't be the first to go. I hope you find the tips, tools, and ideas offered here helpful as you create solid workforce development links to your organization's successful strategic plan.

Karen Mantyla, CDE
President
Quiet Power Inc.
Washington, D.C.
May 2009

The Real Value of Learning

Making the Link to the Bottom Line

Karen Mantyla

Executive Summary

Training budgets get cut for many reasons, and senior-level decision makers are the ones who decide where to cut. How can training professionals develop a plan to change that decision? It all starts with a mindset about training or learning as a whole, especially the mindset of those who make the money decisions—those C-suite decision makers who need to "see" the value of learning and how it links to *their* success and the bottom line of the organization. After reading this chapter, you will understand

■ why learning is undervalued
■ how to begin to change the mindset of decision makers
■ how to meet the challenges of building visibility and respect for learning.

Understanding Why Training Is Often Undervalued

As you will see in the case studies presented in this book, it is possible to change the nature of the conversation and thus the perception of the value of learning.

It is important to understand that the realities faced by learning executives and other training professionals can be daunting:

- Learning is not seen as a bottom-line-producing investment. Senior business executives and other top decision makers often do not know how to link learning to organizational success. It becomes *your* job to make that link for them.
- Training executives are not often invited to participate in budget discussions because they are perceived as lacking enterprise knowledge, a strategic mindset, ever-changing organizational knowledge, business skills, communication skills, or understanding the need to be proactive.
- Solid metrics to measure the true value of learning have not been clearly defined and tracked. Consequently, top management does not see the value.
- Training courses, events, and activities are often scheduled as a reaction to assessed gaps in performance, resulting in training being seen as reactive rather than proactive. From this perspective, management often sees training as a cost and a possible drain on resources, rather than as a strategic value-added investment to achieve its goals. Ask yourself: How often are your individual development plans (IDPs) linked to the business plan and the strategic goals?

Along with these challenges, there are additional factors, which I call failure factors, that left unaddressed will lead to major problems in establishing the value of learning with decision makers in the organization (see sidebar). The experiences of the organizations presented in this book give concrete lessons for meeting these failure factors head on.

Failure Factors

- Limited or no knowledge of the enterprise strategic plan
- Limited business acumen among learning professionals
- Training courses or events that have no tie-in to enterprise strategy
- Weak business relationships with senior decision makers
- Workforce development team members who do not attend enterprise strategy sessions
- Little or no alignment with the training needs of every part of the enterprise
- No workforce development plan with evaluation and metrics tied to ROI
- Doing things the same way because that's what has been done before
- Failure to communicate the value and impact of learning to the bottom line
- Lack of effective persuasion and presentation skills
- No buy-in from senior leaders for workforce development plan
- Lack of effective planning, evaluation, and measurement impact to the bottom line

---

Changing the Mindset

Without a significant change in the mindset at the C level about how workplace learning directly supports strategic goals and contributes to an organization's bottom-line goals, the following statements will continue to be familiar to workplace learning professionals:

- "Other" things take center stage for dollar allocation during times of change and shifting priorities. For example, equipment and other functional areas often take a higher priority as "needs."
- Training and learning are not bottom-line-producing investments.
- Training executives are not invited into strategic budgeting sessions.
- Training events and learning activities are often scheduled to react to the results of a gap in performance rather than proactive strategic alignment with the enterprise goals and priorities.

Can this mindset be changed? Absolutely. It is being accomplished by many people who have learned what they need to do and how they need to do it, and understand how the people making the decisions think. Remember, *people make decisions, organizations don't.* Throughout this book are tips and recommendations, starting with this section, to help *you* help *them* succeed. This chapter and those that follow will show you how to change the conversation with those at the C level by first examining how three world-class organizations and one large governmental agency put learning at the center of their organizational strategy. In addition to these stories of success, this book provides you with some basic tools to create your own success stories.

And a major step toward that success is to begin changing the way those who make the money decisions about learning think. You've got to understand the people, their position, their influence, and how they work to meet the bottom-line goals of the organization. You must learn how to

- Get to know decision makers.
- Get them prepared to "get it."
- Get out there—networking and visibility.
- Get to know your changing organization.
- Get ready to act.

Get to Know Decision Makers

Every decision maker and every learner is different and has a different behavior style at work. In chapter 8, Craig Mindrum offers an in-depth discussion about learning styles, tying them directly to the success of organizational goals and strategy. You can use these principles when communicating with a decision maker. For example, if a decision maker likes to make decisions quickly, you should offer a few strong, attention-grabbing, bottom-line points and be prepared to back up your statements with data. A logical and detail-oriented decision maker likes to see a step-by-step approach backed up with details, charts, and data-mining research. Other C-level executives get frustrated with too many details. Your chances of selling your plan improve if you prepare and communicate based on the particular learning styles of your leaders.

Get Them Prepared to "Get It"

In many instances, senior executives are not aware of the critical link between learning and the bottom line. And when they don't get it, learning budget items get cut. Helping those in the executive suite understand the link begins with a training budget aligned with an integrated, strategic workforce development plan, which in turn is aligned with an enterprisewide strategic plan. The solid line from your plan to the bottom line has to be *clearly visible throughout the year.* When the budget discussions happen, your rock-solid plan has to speak for itself. If it can't, your budget is fair game to be cut.

Get Out There—Networking and Visibility

That old saying "It's who you know" is an old saying because it has merit. Those who have a "known" factor—those who are viewed as important players in the enterprise—are the squeaky wheel that gets the grease. Are you viewed as an important player? If not, this book will show you the elements needed to create your workforce development plan and build this visibility.

For now, here are some top-line suggestions to consider:

- **Use business terminology tied to the bottom line.** Offer to lead groups for needs assessment input—teams, divisions, and so forth. Make sure the words you use reflect those in the strategic plan of your organization, from planning to delivery to reinforcement of your initiatives and actions. The more you align your communications with those in the plan, the more people will begin to realize that learning is tied to their success, as well as that of the organization.
- **Conduct or establish focus groups in conjunction with your learning development activities.** Include key decision makers and operational leaders as valued participants for input and feedback.
- **Ensure that your leadership efforts are visible.** Use a variety of media including webinars, communities of practice, town hall meetings, internal

newsletters, and special links in learning portals. Are you linked to knowledge of the enterprise and learning alignment?

- **Speak at local business association meetings, write a column, or contribute to your local newspaper.** When your words, whether written or verbalized, can reinforce personal, professional, and organizational success, people will take notice.

Get to Know Your Changing Organization

Every organization goes through constant change and rearranging priorities. Make sure your learning plans align with the ever-changing needs of the enterprise. Consider the following in your plan:

- What are the ongoing needs of the organization?
- How do changes affect the different divisions within the organization?
- How do the changes affect the teams within the divisions?
- How do the changes affect the supporting individuals (employees and contractors)?
- How do you keep apprised of ongoing change?

Identify the business goals of each level and operation within your organization, and align them with your recommendations for training investments. Ensure that you link each budget item to a specific strategic goal of the enterprise. Keep a pulse on the ongoing needs of the enterprise decision makers. Because change is constant, keep a pulse on changing priorities and define your own "service plan" and contact intervals for all internal customers.

Get Ready to Act

Anticipating the changing business needs and goals of your organization is vital. Be ready to

- quickly create, design, and deliver just-in-time training for current or changing priorities
- link to the changing priorities of the enterprise, along with documented ROI benefits
- put forth cost-effective training requests based on your target learner population
- use the best possible technology distribution methods for distributed learning and communication
- adapt or change course to meet current needs.

Putting It All Together

Challenges remain at all levels within organizations to prove the value of learning, according to a 2006 Accenture survey of 285 senior learning executives from around the world (Balaguer, Higgins, and Mindrum 2006). These challenges include

- aligning activities with the most pressing and important business or operational needs
- measuring effectiveness and impact on the performance of the business or agency as a whole
- proactively communicating value to all stakeholders
- earning acceptance of the learning function across the leadership of the entire enterprise.

But, as you will see in the Accenture case study in the next chapter, it is possible to move past these challenges. Accenture's experience provides an inspiring roadmap of how to position learning for success: "Rigorous ROI studies can convince decision makers that investments they make in learning and workforce performance translate into improved business performance" (Balaguer, Higgins, and Mindrum 2006). Such studies can also, from the other side of the equation, alert decision makers to potential negative impacts on the business if they do not make such investments.

Learning must be on a straight line to the bottom line. Once you build your case, present it well and discuss strategic learning. What C-level decision maker wants to jeopardize the realization of achieving strategic goals? This mindset shift to incorporating learning as a key driver to achieve business goals is the place you want to be.

■ ■ ■

Leveraging the Learning Advantage

This chapter explores the real value of learning and the very best ways to communicate and leverage that value in your organization. Here is how you can put these concepts to work for you and your organization:

- Know, understand, and be able to verbalize the strategic plan of your organization.
- Develop business relationships with the key decision makers.
- Understand the power of the mindset and how to change it, if needed.

- Master the business skills necessary to speak in bottom-line terms and alignment.
- Ensure that your persuasion and communication skills are sharp.
- Take responsibility for visibility and business networking at the top.
- Ensure that your needs assessment of the employees spans every level and operation within the organization.
- Monitor the pulse of the needs of the decision makers and the managers of all key operations.
- Deal with change as part of your plan.

Transforming Learning at Accenture

Driving High Performance with Strategic Technology-Supported Learning Programs

Don Vanthournout,
Chief Learning Officer, Accenture,
and Kurt J. Olson,
Director of Capability Solutions, Accenture

Executive Summary

In response to new business challenges, Accenture launched an enterprise learning transformation program focused on employee development and providing value for the company. This was accomplished, in part, by gaining support from company executives and linking the vision of the learning transformation program to Accenture's corporate values.

Use of the V-Model for Learning and Knowledge Management helped identify performance needs and determine cost-effective responses. In addition, maintaining a focus on "phenomenal" learning, creating a comprehensive learning infrastructure, and developing a two-level approach to governance, leadership, and sponsorship have positioned Accenture to continue enabling its employees to develop professionally on an ongoing basis.

Recognizing a Need for Transformation

Over the past several years, Accenture, one of the world's leading management consulting, technology services, and outsourcing companies, has experienced a dramatic transformation, spurred by one of the most challenging times in the history of the company—indeed, in the recent history of the global economy. Faced with worldwide economic turmoil following the bursting of the Internet bubble, the broad effects of global terrorism, the rapidly changing needs of corporations and governments (our clients), and increased margin pressures, Accenture's long-standing commitment to the development of its people was being challenged as never before.

And our people were noticing. Some requests for training were being denied because of the tremendous pressure to serve clients. Employee satisfaction scores were dipping. For a company like Accenture, which really sells knowledge and experience—business value delivered through people—this was cause for great concern.

Our response was a broad organizational transformation program focused on our people and their development. At the same time, it was a transformation of how we envisioned, designed, delivered, and operated training. No longer was it acceptable to view learning as a cost center; we had to prove that it added value to the company. Moreover, we had to operate the learning function more efficiently and rigorously, with one eye on the bottom line and the other on the value being created for the company.

The enterprise learning transformation program at Accenture has had measurable effects at several levels. We have successfully aligned our learning strategy with Accenture's business strategy and significantly upgraded our core curricula to meet today's needs in each of Accenture's workforces. Our employee engagement scores have risen, and our courses are rated highly. Anyone glancing through our course evaluation results will see the positive effects of this learning transformation program. Learning at Accenture is changing people's lives; it's giving them more reason than ever to stay with us and grow both personally and professionally.

Equally impressive have been the cost efficiencies Accenture has gained by leveraging advanced learning technologies and by running learning like a business. Accenture is receiving more return on its investment today than at the beginning of its learning transformation. Today's training budget, though very healthy, is 7 percent less than it was five years ago (11 percent less, taking inflation into consideration), even though Accenture is now training a workforce that is 67 percent larger.

Enterprise learning has significantly contributed to Accenture's journey toward high performance. Our learning transformation was successful, in part, because of our ability to execute a series of projects involving both hard and soft skills. This propelled the company's learning capabilities through advanced technologies; measurement programs and operational excellence; and activities involving executive sponsorship, governance, and change management.

Creating a Vision

A journey of a thousand miles begins with a single step, as the ancient Chinese proverb says. In the case of an organization initiating a transformational change program focused on learning and workforce performance, that first step is visualizing and then planning for the final destination. It involves creating an enterprisewide vision of how the initiative will reshape the company through new capabilities, and then planning and putting in place the right team to make that vision a reality.

Across industries, organizational transformation programs have a fairly low success rate. Many reasons lie behind such failures. Some factors lie outside the control of change leaders, such as economic downturns or a reassignment of key executive leadership midway through the program. In many cases, however, failure can be traced back to the beginning—to overlooking or giving short shrift to a number of visioning and planning activities. For us, critical activities included achieving executive buy-in, presenting a clear business case for the transformation program, choosing the right team, and aligning the vision with the core values of the enterprise as a whole.

Inspiring Conviction

Early in the planning phase for our learning transformation program, the chief executive of one of our operating groups provided a succinct and powerful summary of the challenge ahead: "Your goal is to make enterprise learning one of the top three priorities that our executive group, especially the CEO, is working on. If your program is not on the short list of top priorities, it will be very difficult to get executive attention and buy-in."

Key to making learning a top-three priority among our leaders was taking the time to meet with as many of them one-on-one as we could. During those meetings, executives discovered that many of their presumptions about the current state of learning and training at Accenture were no longer true. Most of these senior executives had, themselves, been through the core training program at Accenture that, during the years when they began their careers, had stressed a common curriculum and a shared experience and enculturation at a central training facility located just outside of Chicago.

The commitment to a common curriculum and the award-winning training programs developed by the company at that time meant that a client could walk into an Accenture office in Chicago, London, Manila, Buenos Aires, or any of Accenture's offices in the 49 countries in which it now operates, and find almost uniform levels of competence among employees, as well as a stable, consistent approach to executing a technology, strategy, or outsourcing project. It meant that a client could ask anyone on a project team—the newest hire to the most senior executive—about the purpose and progress of the work and get a good sense of where things stood: what the goals and vision were, what distinctive value was being created, what milestones had been reached, what work remained, and how that person's role and tasks fit into the whole.

No one ever set out to kill the core training curriculum. But through a series of tactical decisions, shared training had faded away. Different groups at Accenture had been empowered over the years to develop their own training for their own specific needs. That seemed like a good business decision at the time. But a consequence was that the common curriculum on which Accenture had once built a shared sense of culture and purpose had eroded over time.

So during our initial meetings with our senior executives, we showed each of them a chart of the mainline training courses that they had been through themselves as younger professionals. We asked them if this was still how they understood the Accenture training curriculum. When they answered affirmatively, we opened the chart up to its full size to show them the reality. From a shared core of more than a dozen courses offered to employees in the 1980s and 1990s, the core had shrunk to two courses: an introductory course for analysts (the term given to new employees) and a seminar for newly promoted executives. The senior executives were shocked.

Those meetings did more than just give our leaders information; they inspired conviction among them that change was needed and that their personal involvement would be critical to the success of the learning transformation program.

Choosing the Right Team

The core leadership team in the Capability Development group—those involved in planning and executing the learning transformation program—was really more of a business team focused on corporate education than it was an education team trying to have a business impact. A number of us had performed client work at Accenture for many years before joining the Capability Development organization. Others had specific expertise in such areas as technology, methodology, and performance measurement.

It's not that we were no longer committed to developing great, leading-edge training. Quite the contrary. Continuing the distinguished tradition of Accenture's training organization was one of the key goals of the transformation. But in the end, identifying great ideas for learning design and delivery is not the hardest part of what a learning executive does. The biggest challenges are managing those great ideas toward positive business results and aligning investments with business strategy with sufficient rigor to earn the trust of executive leadership. Hence, putting together a team with the right business experience and program management skills was vital.

Our core team included experienced business people in areas such as learning strategy, curriculum planning and development, training operations, and technology development. Once the team members were assembled, we made an effort to inspire conviction in them, too. In effect, we were asking them to take a risk: Put your professional backgrounds on the line to see if, together, we can successfully transform the training situation at Accenture.

Aligning the Vision with the Company's Core Values

The strongest buildings sink their foundations deep into the ground. Similarly, the strongest visions are founded on the deep cultural and social values of a company. The Capability Development group tied the overall vision for learning transformation to the publicly stated core values of Accenture: stewardship, best people, client value creation, respect for the individual, integrity, and one global network.

We also linked the vision to the leadership model at Accenture. This model emphasizes three important components of leadership: value creation for the company, people developers on behalf of the workforce, and business operators who are effective stewards of company resources. Aligning our vision and plans to our corporate values and to our own leadership model was an important success factor. It gave us a structure and based our work on what we value most and what those values mean for how we lead our people. And it resonated with Accenture senior executives, helping to secure their ongoing commitment.

Of course, even the best visions and plans must be followed immediately by effective execution. But the right vision—created, planned, and reinforced the right way—can become a beacon for the challenging journey of organizational transformation.

Maximizing the Return on Learning

One of the most important trends in enterprise learning today is the ever-sharpening focus on linking corporate training programs to the business. Recent

Accenture learning research into high-performance learning organizations, based on a survey of 285 senior learning executives around the world, found that maximizing the impact of learning on the business was the number one challenge of learning executives—more vexing, even, than dealing with budget constraints.

What makes it so challenging? The enterprise learning organization must transform from cost center to value center, explicitly linking its spending on training programs to overall business value created. This linkage involves two important objectives:

1. Focusing measurement on performance—that is, ensuring that the results of training are measured not just in terms of the numbers of courses developed or how many employees have been trained, but also in terms of the impact of those courses on people's performance
2. Creating and delivering learning assets with business rigor—developing them on time and on budget, and delivering them in the most cost-efficient manner possible.

The executives overseeing Accenture's internal training function were focused on both of these objectives as they sought to transform the company's internal training programs. Accenture had a rich heritage of developing award-winning training. On top of those expectations, however, executives needed to instill operational effectiveness into training development. World-class training was still the goal, but so was rigorous program management that operated within strict budget and time constraints to deliver maximum business impact with maximum cost efficiency.

Our learning transformation team did a number of things to impress on our leadership the fact that their investments would pay off in ways with measurable impact on the business. For example, we conducted an award-winning ROI study, including the development of a university-endorsed economic model, which proved that, even in its current state, training was delivering triple-digit returns on Accenture's investments—353 percent, to be exact.

Equally important, we then set out to ensure that we had a way to clearly link training projects with specific business objectives during the planning phase, communicate these plans clearly to sponsors, and then guide designers during the development process. The team achieved those goals by adapting a tool from Accenture's core systems building methodology to create a unique and innovative asset, the Accenture V-Model for Learning and Knowledge Management (see figure 2-1).

As a systems development asset repurposed for the development of learning and knowledge assets, the model's focus on testing rigor translates into precise specification of performance outcomes expected from training development. The V-Model

Figure 2-1. The Accenture V-Model for Learning and Knowledge Management

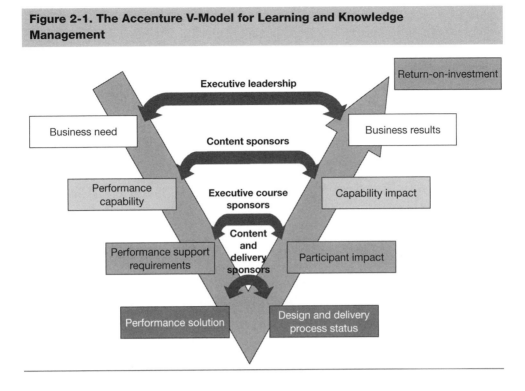

links business needs to the specific outcomes of the learning assets to be developed and provides a framework for measuring results across all levels of delivery—from deployment of the solution through ROI. The full metrics architecture conforms to leading practices in training evaluation. And, because the model comprises the entire performance space, it facilitates a crucial shift needed by enterprise learning organizations today: from a focus on the traditional "training is the solution for everything" approach to the more precise development of learning and knowledge solutions appropriate to real performance needs.

The Accenture V-Model for Learning and Knowledge Management

The V-Model drives a process that proceeds from macro-level analysis through finer specification of detail. First, the model clearly defines the business problem or opportunity. At the same time, the model specifies the business impact metrics. Once captured and compared to cost, these metrics will help determine return on overall investment.

This reflective analysis—identifying requirements and metrics simultaneously—proceeds level by level down the model. For example, the business need is met by developing a performance capability, which is enabled by developing individual human performance support, which is enabled by the learning and/or knowledge solution. The left side of the model maps the stages of analysis that ultimately result in the design and deployment of a solution that is linked to the original business goal. In these stages, the business need is translated into capability requirements, human performance requirements, and, finally, into solution designs.

The right side of the model maps the metrics used to evaluate success at each of these levels. Business impact and ROI metrics are specified near the top, with implementation and individual outcomes near the bottom. The pattern and correlation of metrics between levels provide insight about particular obstacles that might impede success. Or, when business results are demonstrated, the model provides evidence of the unique impact of the solution on those results.

Benefits of the Model

The key to the effectiveness of the V-Model is its symmetry. On the left side, representing analysis of learning needs and the design of solutions, the model requires that a development team also create the metrics that will link the plans with its associated results. This helps ensure tight linkages between the analysis/design phase and the measurement phase.

The model also ensures that the right sponsors and decision makers (see the middle of the "V") get the metrics and results that mean the most to them. Those who serve as sponsors for a particular learning offering will be most interested in metrics that indicate how successfully that course was administered and the impact it had on participants. Those who ask for particular business content to be reflected in a set of courses (for example, because of a marketplace need in serving customers) want to see the impact of the learning experience on workforce capabilities. And executive leadership wants to see the business results emerging from the overall learning environment.

A Focus on Performance Needs

In most traditional training organizations, formal courses are most often presumed to be the solution to a workforce performance need, and then the training planners work backward to connect the solution to need. That can be an expensive and wasteful approach.

Instead, the Accenture V-Model provides guidance to learning and knowledge development—planning, developing, delivering, and communicating—without starting from the position that formal training will always be the right answer. Formal training is expensive and, thus, should be a thoughtful response instead of an automatic one, used only when it will clearly meet the business need. Often, the best response to an identified workforce need is not formal training; it might be something to improve employee motivation, knowledge sharing, mentoring, or other performance supports.

The essential focus of an enterprise learning organization should be, first, to identify the performance needs in the workforce, and then to determine the appropriate responses through an analysis mapped to measurable results within the organization's budget and resource constraints. When used properly to guide the development of training solutions, the V-Model results in solutions closely linked to business needs, and metrics that are tied to performance objectives.

Phenomenal Learning

What about the quality of the training itself? An important moment for our team came when, during a meeting early in the change program, our global HR lead made the following statement: "Whatever else we do, the learning programs we create have to be phenomenal." The "phenomenal" label as the summary vision for learning design and delivery at Accenture caught on. For us, it came to mean, "creating a surprising and delighting level of excellence in every aspect of the training experience." This shifted the focus of learning design in an important way. The question for the learning transformation leadership team became, what else can we do to create a learning experience here that has the potential to change someone's career—even change someone's life? For those employees already satisfied with their work, what can we do to make them feel even better about working for Accenture? And for those whose commitment to the company is wavering, how might a positive training experience make them want to stay?

Delivering phenomenal learning, we now argue, involves a focus on four interrelated dimensions: learning, networking, enculturation, and the guest experience. That is, in addition to the experience of the training program itself, effective enterprise learning needs to build in opportunities to network with colleagues and with senior leaders of the organization. There needs to be adequate attention paid to how the learning experience reflects the organizational culture and how it can help draw people in and engage them in that culture. Finally, the training needs to treat employees with the same kind of care and respect that a hotel might give its guests.

Let's face it, too few organizations think of their employees this way. But what we have tried to do with our on-site courses, for example, is to give our employees a first-class experience every step of the way: their experience checking into their rooms at the start of training, the meals they are served and the way they are served, the professionalism of the presentations, and the technology used. Electronic learning can be phenomenal, too, with attention paid to how the experience is designed and delivered. Especially as organizations around the world begin competing for talent more aggressively, we believe that delivering phenomenal learning will be a key part of engaging employees in the life and culture of the organization.

Using Technology to Create a High-Performance Learning Organization

At the beginning of this transformational journey, the technology infrastructure for learning at Accenture—once considered state of the art—had grown old and less reliable. Its technology base was in a shape similar to many companies today: fragmented, with information distributed over hundreds of databases worldwide. That situation raised distressing data integrity issues, and it also made it difficult to run centralized compliance reports or assess the value delivered from internal training. Managing any of the information centrally was time consuming and required a great deal of manual support, so the learning infrastructure had also become very expensive.

Accenture faced the risk that its existing learning infrastructure would not hold up well under the strain of the broader transformation program. Our learning strategy, for example, called for more e-learning to support development of Accenture professionals. We wanted to be able to support more rapid development and delivery and empower our people to manage their own learning plans.

The answer, our team knew, was to create a single learning infrastructure; however, this would be a significant technical challenge. It meant retiring local systems and creating one learning management system, one virtual instructor-led system, and one learning data warehouse for all of Accenture across dozens of countries and hundreds of business units. Yet this was part of the vision driving the entire transformation team: Use technology in the most effective way possible to provide exceptional learning experiences, track learning delivery and results, and provide the information needed to support effective decision making about how to best steer the learning function in the long term.

Creating an Effective Team

As with our entire transformation program, choosing the right team to lead the infrastructure aspects was critical. We chose business architects and charged them with ensuring that all investments were properly targeted to the right business needs and goals. This team, when assembled, had two key strengths: (1) a balance of both business savvy and technical know-how; and (2) the desire to use technology not for technology's sake, but toward the goal of developing a learning infrastructure that will have a measurable, positive effect on how Accenture's people learn and work.

The governance role played by this team was important to achieving the goals of the overall learning transformation program. A critical factor in the team's success was identifying an advocate for each of the key stakeholders: business sponsors and management, as well as employees. The team included someone responsible for the personalization of the learning infrastructure and another individual responsible for reporting. In addition, a particularly innovative step was to assign another team member responsibility for the experience of the learners themselves. With this team makeup, Accenture had more assurance that technology would be applied to meet the needs of all stakeholders.

A Comprehensive Learning Infrastructure

The global learning management system ultimately delivered for Accenture is called "myLearning." It coordinates the work of the decentralized business units to provide the following:

- Intuitive access to comprehensive information resources that enable Accenture professionals to be effective consumers of education, based on both the company's and the individual's needs.
- Common, standardized delivery platforms for distributed education to reach Accenture employees closer to the job site, to minimize delivery costs, and to allow the operating groups and business units to focus on education content instead of technical delivery.
- Common, consistent feedback from all learning assets to proactively manage the quality of the content delivered to Accenture employees.
- Comprehensive reporting to improve management decision making and better align the overall education investment with business need.

Because of myLearning, all of Accenture's employees today—more than 180,000 people in 49 countries—can go to a single intranet site for their learning and development needs. The new system created a single shared infrastructure for all virtual learning, one survey system to measure learning effectiveness, and one central data warehouse and decision support system for tracking and reporting. Deploying a global learning management system was, in fact, a critical factor in the entire success story of reinventing learning at Accenture. Retiring all the local training management systems allowed us to redeploy the associated local administrative personnel, representing more than $23 million in cost avoidance in the first three years and contributing to strong executive support for the business case. In terms of ongoing costs, the myLearning capabilities enable Accenture to effectively track actual course usage to optimize vendor contracts—that is, to determine costs on actual course completion, not just on course availability.

The new system also incorporates a decision support function, which integrates information from a variety of sources and provides a customized, comprehensive, and timely snapshot of learning metrics. This reporting function is essential for the company's learning professionals, as well as its business executives.

The proper application of technology to Accenture's learning design and delivery capabilities has resulted in more timely and relevant support for the company's different workforces across industries. The global training team can more effectively plan courses that meet business needs and do so in ways that also create compelling learning experiences for the company's employees. Training delivered via e-learning or online seminars can be integrated into the holistic picture of career development and learning for the company. And executives can use reporting from the global learning management system to make more informed decisions about helping employees work together toward the common goal of achieving high performance.

More recently, Accenture has begun to blend knowledge-sharing activities with its enterprise learning programs. Today's workers really don't care if the support they are receiving is "training" or "knowledge management." All that's important is that they have the information and skill building they need to serve clients effectively and to grow personally.

The new Accenture Knowledge Exchange gives Accenture employees around the world instant access to an improved system for organizing, accessing, and sharing knowledge and experience. One of the innovations at this development stage was leveraging the existing capabilities of the myLearning infrastructure to create an enterprise search capability, common across Accenture's content delivery tools.

A More Effective Strategic Sourcing Strategy for Learning Design and Delivery

Until the time of this learning transformation program, Accenture, like most organizations, used its own dedicated team of employees to create proprietary learning content, support the execution of its classroom training program, and maintain the learning infrastructure for the company. Now, to maximize cost efficiency, Accenture intended to develop and then follow a more sophisticated approach to strategic sourcing of learning design and delivery.

There are many strategic dimensions to learning that an organization such as Accenture generally intends to keep in-house. However, for more transactional and delivery functions, companies do well to automate where possible, then pursue shared services and outsourcing models—not just for cost and efficiency reasons, but also to leverage the expertise of a provider whose core competency lies within the business function being outsourced.

By outsourcing key administration, design, and delivery capabilities to Accenture Learning (Accenture's learning outsourcing business unit), the company's central training could benefit from the kind of efficiency that often results only from a supplier-to-customer relationship. The Accenture team retained its key planning functions in-house, while also benefiting from the consultation of Accenture Learning. This way, the internal team could continue to determine the learning strategy and objectives, define the curricula, and shape specific courses and solutions. It could then turn to its outsourcing partner to design, build, and deliver those learning programs in a manner that balanced quality with cost effectiveness.

Better sourcing and vendor management is one way that training organizations can improve their ability to "run learning like a business." Senior management in every industry increasingly measures the performance of learning executives in terms of how well they manage the business side of learning and how well they meet defined business outcomes. By infusing a learning team with sound business skills and program management techniques, and by leveraging the right use of key technologies and sourcing strategies, enterprise learning can increase a company's ability to achieve high performance.

Role of Governance and Leadership in Learning Transformation

A distinctive characteristic of any organizational transformation program is that it takes time—often several years if high performance is to be achieved and sustained. That long-term journey poses a number of risks, especially for an enterprise learning transformation.

Many interests and goals compete for the attention of any senior executive team. During a multiyear learning transformation program, the gains made during preliminary phases of work might be undermined in later phases if executive commitment wanes or if attention is overly diverted to other initiatives. Ensuring that senior leadership is on board for the long haul is one of the key goals of the leadership and governance dimensions of enterprise learning transformation.

Executive commitment to long-term change does not happen by accident. With careful planning about governance, leadership, and sponsorship structures, including an advanced approach to configuring the executive steering committee, companies stand a better chance of successfully managing the journey of enterprise learning transformation.

Governance, Leadership, and Sponsorship at Two Levels

The Accenture team took an innovative approach to ensure that governance structures and sponsorship initiatives for the change program were instituted at two levels. The resources of a training organization are not limitless; hard choices must be made about initiatives that can and cannot be supported within budget constraints. So governance must be focused not only at a broad and high level—ensuring the ongoing commitment and involvement of the executives who control budgets and business priorities—but also at a more detailed level, focused on those more directly involved in detailed business strategies and the training necessary to make those strategies successful.

Level-One Governance: The Executive Steering Committee

The steering committee put in place to lead and sponsor a major change program must reflect the unique reporting and go-to-market structures of the organization and include all its major stakeholders. Accenture goes to market primarily through what it calls "operating groups"—groups with deep skills and experience in particular industries and subindustries. In addition, "capability groups" provide specialized skills to clients in such areas as customer relationship management, human performance, and finance. The chief executives for each of the five operating groups, as well as the leads for the capability groups, were appointed to the steering committee for the learning transformation program, as well as Accenture's chief leadership officer, chief learning officer, and global HR lead.

The types and frequency of meetings of a steering committee will change as the transformation program proceeds. At the beginning of the Accenture program, meetings often were held in person as the team hammered out the strategy. At the start of any transformation program, personal interaction is absolutely critical to successful governance. The committee members must do more than discuss official strategy documents sanctioned by top executives; they need to hear those strategies come to life in the actual words of the company's top stakeholders.

"Sponsorship" is the key goal usually mentioned in any effective governance program for a major change initiative. However, in the case of Accenture's learning transformation program, we were after more than cheerleading. We sought active participation. That approach proved important as the global economy worsened during the change program. Although some in the company at that time advocated cutting back on learning services temporarily, the group chief executives—who by then were sponsors of Accenture's primary or core training schools—said no: For the company to continue serving clients well by conducting innovative and high-quality work, the company's people had to be at the leading edge of their fields.

That experience underscores another important point about effective steering committees: The members stick to their plans and promises, and they use their clout wisely, when needed, to push past resistance. For example, at one point in the Accenture change program, a decision was made to alter the sequence of early-career training, requiring a refocus of investments to get a particular group of 3,600 employees on the right sequence. It was an expensive decision, one that meant some other areas of the company would temporarily lose their training budgets. When this happened, having a strong steering committee made it easier for the internal training and HR organization. We did not need to convince hundreds of people about the decision. Instead, we just said that the group chief executives supported the decision. Constructive contrary opinions are always welcome, of course. But when hard decisions must be made, the executive steering committee must be prepared to be accountable for its decisions—and stick with them.

Level-Two Governance: Executive Sponsors for Training Courses

A key to the success of Accenture's learning transformation program was a second level of governance put in place to drive the creation of learning content that was closely linked to the company's most current business objectives. This second level was achieved by designating executive sponsors for each training course in the evolving curriculum. In most cases, these sponsors were also members of the steering committee, which gave them an additional personal ownership in the quality of the new learning experiences being designed.

This second level of governance strengthened the connection between the learning organization and the needs of Accenture's business. Ideally, the learning organization creates the product while giving the business owners responsibility for designing what the product should look like. Consider an analogy to auto manufacturing: One group designates what a car should look like based on market needs and consumer research, and another group produces the car with high quality and at the right price. With training, the business owners are in charge of designating what training is required for particular business needs, but the training organization applies its specialty skills to create high-quality training within budget constraints.

Involving those business owners in an ongoing manner is critical to achieving the best return on learning. One particular method used by the training content development team was to begin with one-page summary documents for each career level of the Accenture workforce. The goal of the executive in charge of each major content area was to summarize on that single page what the performance outcomes needed to be as employees progressed through various career levels. Subsequently, this work led to the creation of a more detailed curriculum framework.

With the involvement of the sponsors, decisions were made more readily about what type of training experience would be most effective for the lowest cost. With the right governance system in place for content design and delivery, the team effectively gave the content decisions to the school sponsors who were closest to the need. However, they maintained control over how the content would be delivered to maximize the effectiveness of the experience while also staying within cost constraints.

This two-tiered system of governance and sponsorship is vital to keeping a learning transformation program on track to achieving high performance. The approach engages top leadership and helps ensure their ongoing commitment; at the same time, it involves senior executives in the right way in the myriad decisions that must be made at a lower level to deliver phenomenal learning experiences in a cost-conscious manner.

High Performance Delivered

No matter how successful a transformational change program is, there is always one sobering fact to bear in mind: The journey is never over. Certainly there have been times when the Accenture team has been able to step back and celebrate its accomplishments. But there is little time to rest in such a competitive industry. Today, Accenture is moving on in its relentless quest for high performance, finding new ways to enable its global workforce, connect employees to each other, align their performance with business needs, and give them an opportunity to bring their innovations to bear upon the success of the company.

The transformation at Accenture has had a big effect on the people of the company and its culture. And, as noted earlier, we have delivered impressive and ongoing cost benefits to the company. Beyond the immediate effects of learning that one can see and experience is a host of other effects. Accenture has stepped up to fulfill the promise it makes to those who join the company: to commit to their professional development, to give them world-class opportunities in both work and learning, and to commit to their growth in both good economic times and bad. There is growing pride as Accenture increasingly wins awards and recognition for its work in learning and knowledge management. This external validation is additional assurance that things are moving in the right direction.

The enterprise learning transformation at Accenture is vivid evidence of how learning and other workforce enablement programs help drive high performance for an entire organization. The journey is never over, but we have measurable evidence that by reinventing learning at Accenture, we have had a positive impact on the performance of our business.

■ ■ ■

Leveraging the Learning Advantage

- When planning a learning transformation program for an organization, it is important to
  - Win long-term support from the top executives
  - Assemble a business-savvy team who can successfully manage learning design and delivery
  - Link the vision of the learning transformation to the organization's core values and leadership model
  - Show that the learning transformation program will result in a positive ROI and improved employee performance.
- Employing a tool such as Accenture's V-Model for Learning and Knowledge Management can help identify critical business goals and the performance needs of the workforce, and then determine the appropriate cost-effective responses.
- "Phenomenal" training creates surprising, delighting levels of excellence in every aspect of the training experience by focusing on learning, networking, enculturation, and the guest experience.
- A single learning infrastructure, such as Accenture's myLearning, allows intuitive access to comprehensive information resources, standardized delivery platforms, consistent feedback, and comprehensive reporting.
- Training organizations can improve their ability to "run learning like a business" through better sourcing and vendor management.

- A two-level governance program is recommended:
    - At the first level, an executive steering committee drives sponsorship throughout the organization and helps ensure ongoing support and commitment to investments.
    - At the second level, executive sponsors for training courses strengthen the connection between the learning organization and the needs of the business.
- Learning should be positioned as a strategic function, not an operational one. This requires sustained commitment, time, and energy from company senior executives. It also requires business people running the learning function (that is, the CLO and the leadership team) who understand both the business world and the learning world. They bridge the two worlds and translate the business requirements into appropriate learning programs for their teams to execute. This learning leadership team must also commit to developing a high-performing learning function, one that becomes a high-performing group through a commitment to excellence, the discipline to focus only on top-priority programs, and alignment with the vision/core values of the organization.

■ ■ ■ **3**

Blending Technology, Learning, and Strategy

The Ultimate End Game

Karen Mantyla

Executive Summary

The ultimate learning blend for the 21st century includes reliance on technology and a strong link to strategy. One element alone will not lead to great success—but a combination strengthens the achievements of all. Strategy is the roadmap; learning equips a workforce with the skills and competencies they need to achieve the strategy. With targeted use of technology, we can decide which distribution methods will best serve long- and short-term goals. The case studies will look at these three elements—technology, learning, and strategy—and how integrating them with each other can lead to organizational success. This chapter will address

■ the opportunities presented by blending
■ how to do it right the first time
■ understanding needs assessment.

Learning is a lifetime pursuit for most, whether it be to learn a functional skill or a new recipe. Most of us want to keep up and learn new things for both our personal and professional lives. No one really knows it all—because "all" is a moving target. No matter what age-based generation we're in, we have one thing in common: We have unprecedented access to information and learning. And although the new generation experienced teething on a keyboard, every generation is affected by the capabilities of technology. Take Great Britain's Queen Elizabeth II, for example; she launched her own special Royal Channel on YouTube at the age of 81!

This is an exciting time for technology and learning, and the future will bring still more opportunities to individualize our learning experiences in ways we cannot even imagine. The benefit to organizations is that strategy can be broken down into chunks of learning needs and requirements. Technology can guide us quickly to a result (What have you Googled today?) or take us on an electronic journey to learn new skills logically. With the availability of learning from top universities for free, nearly anyone can listen to lectures, download information, and learn from a new angle. And although the angles are always changing, the bottom line is that technology opens up new ways to get smarter. Having this type of learning access, coupled with the smart use of workplace technology, enables us to become better educated and more productive in our society.

Opportunities for Blending Learning and Technology

Although the world of learning and technology offers many opportunities for blending, the one constant to keep in your line of vision is that learning is learning (and not that technology inevitably leads to learning). The learner must remain the central focus, and learning professionals must identify the competencies needed for strategic success, understand the available technology options and the pros and cons of each, and create design options to meet different learner styles and needs.

The ultimate blend ensures that key result areas align and coordinate with the strategic goals of the enterprise. Making the right choices in a systematic way helps ensure that learning experiences are engaging and learner centered—and that learners can "get it" the first time around.

Technology Options

Technology options are everywhere. The key is not to be blinded by it all, but to look at each technology as a primary ingredient in an overall learning plan. Understanding the technologies and learning possibilities helps ensure that you map the right ones in your plan to achieve the strategic learning goal. For example, blended learning content for multigenerational use needs to be tailored to not only different learning styles but also different paces of learning.

The Internet offers many ways to learn. Whether we Google to learn something new or to validate what we already know, the world of technology is multiplying the ways we can learn and receive content. This has provided an unlimited wealth of information, interaction, and outreach opportunity at our fingertips. Just through this one distribution method, we can have targeted learning delivered in many ways, including webinars, tools, job aids, collaboration, synchronous or asynchronous chats, blogs, guest speakers, communities of practice, and more distribution options yet to be created. The point is that our options have increased tremendously. As we look to align our learning content with our enterprise strategic plan, we want to ensure that our learning strategy uses all of the distribution methods available to us.

In this book, my colleagues and I want to provide ideas and an inside look into the learning and support technologies that others are using, as well as tips to ensure that you can create the blend that is right for you and your organization. Although the number of options can often be overwhelming, the true value of using blended learning with technology-supported options is to help align your learning content to meet the strategic learning needs of the enterprise *at the right time*.

We want to select learning technologies to support the requirements of the learning objectives and tasks. We want to identify the tasks and outcomes needed for learning content, then decide which technologies would best support the needs of our learners. Sometimes we have the technology in-house, sometimes we use external providers, and sometimes we have a combination of both. In my previous book, *Blending E-Learning: The Power Is in the Mix*, there is a step-by-step process with regard to how to effectively select and blend technology (Mantyla 2001).

The bottom line of technology-supported learning is that it will align best with the needs of the learners and the speed of learning needed by the enterprise. If we need to ramp up quickly, there are learning technologies that are best suited for that type of distribution. If we need to demonstrate an intricate procedure or task, there are technology solutions that can help ensure that the learners learn in ways that still meet strategic timelines.

You'll see this situation in the real-world example of the Microsoft Xbox in chapter 4. Michael Hatt, former global training manager for Xbox, was tasked with creating a blended solution to get thousands of people trained in a short time-frame. His use of 3D simulations helped reach strategic and global targets in many different ways. With a great success story like this so early in the game (no pun intended), Hatt and his team created a learning environment that can be accessed from around the world.

With technology constantly being updated with new versions, the people who support the users of the products must be able to keep up with the continual learning that is needed. The launch of the Xbox product Halo3 was an incredible success for Microsoft. Thanks to Hatt and his team, the customer service support personnel ramped up quickly and thoroughly and were ready to provide great service.

No matter our age or level of experience, we're all touched and affected, in some way, by technology and the incredible choices available to us. The goal then is not to get all the latest technological golly-gee-whiz stuff just because it is available, but to use technology to touch our learners in ways that make sense for our organization. We don't need to get mobile devices for every employee to ensure that they can view a podcast whenever or wherever they want. However, if that is what makes sense for the distribution of your learning content, that's a different story. Decisions must be made about using the technologies you currently have, acquiring the new technologies you don't, or outsourcing your technology needs to a vendor partner.

Every organization has different technology options, challenges, and opportunities. The goal, no matter what you have available, is to deliver learning content that is well received, easy to apply, and easy to distribute in the real-world lives of the learners. We know that in a technology-based environment, just as in a classroom environment, we must design to attract and benefit those with different learning styles, an issue addressed more fully in chapter 8 by Craig Mindrum. Mindrum raises the critical awareness of the very nature of blending design options and appropriate technologies to meet diverse learner needs.

We see new technology developments being created every day, and keeping up can be difficult. Yet having a good sense of general practices and good principles in using technology can help us create a blend just like a skilled symphony conductor. When we know the learning strategy we want and need, we then can decide which technologies will produce the best results and hit our enterprise learning targets. As with a symphony, having the right instruments can produce an overall effect and sound that is awesome. But, if the conductor does not include the right instruments, we might end up holding our ears. It's up to you to select the right learning technologies so that your end result is a powerful strategic sound wave to the bottom line.

Chapter 5 presents another look at the right blend, this time from the point of view of the U.S. Department of Labor. When e-learning project manager Michael Gerwitz and his team needed to make critical technology selections, they looked at their available options. In their case study they provide an overview of key learning technologies and share their story of acquiring a learning management system (LMS). Although most large organizations have an LMS, some do not set up their system to fully meet the needs of the learners or exploit the system's capabilities to the fullest. With the right configuration and utilization, an LMS can do much more than just track registrations and completion of training hours. It can actually track ROI. This case study will give you a front-row seat into the challenges and decisions made to get the U.S. Department of Labor's LMS up and running. Making the right decision the first time can save your organization a huge amount of money. That in itself hits the bottom line.

Finding the Right Mix

I saw a cartoon a long time ago that showed a CEO sitting behind a big desk. He was telling someone in front of his desk, "The competition uses distance learning. I don't know what it is, but I want two of them." That picture speaks volumes about being knowledgeable (or not) with regard to the current state of using learning technologies. It's a real challenge not only to keep up with all of the hardware and software options but also to select the right ones for the right blend. The right blend means that you are carefully selecting learning distribution channels to deliver chunked learning content that will support and energize all learning styles and all generations within your workforce. That's a tall order.

Some organizations are accomplishing this extremely well (the case studies in this book illustrate this fact); some are doing it but not very well (blending boring, lecture-based, little-interactive content with technology distribution channels that are not very well suited); and still others are not doing it at all.

Decisions about blended learning should not be made without a thorough understanding about the different technologies, their applications, the pros and cons of each, the interactivity options available with each, and benchmarking with others who have used these different technologies. It's also vital that designers and trainers experience learning from each technology-supported learning option selected. Having a focus group of learners who have different learning styles, are multigenerational, and are culturally diverse can offer a real-world perspective to help you get it right the first time. This blend of learners is an important focus to consider before finalizing design and technology distribution options.

We certainly would not expect every CEO or senior officer to have knowledge of all the different technologies available. Yet they expect *us* to be knowledgeable, be aware of what's available, and understand how the enterprise will benefit from the use of technology in our learning initiatives. And, as noted above, getting it right the first time is critical, because wrong decisions can be devastating to the bottom line. Wrong decisions about technology can be seen in wasted money, less-than-acceptable learner value and interest, and loss of confidence in us by those in the C suite.

At one time or another, you have likely experienced an unengaging e-learning event (listening to someone drone on and on). This is often caused by poorly designed interactive learning. Sometimes the use of the wrong technology is the culprit. Learners lose confidence in receiving learning when selections are made that don't make sense. As we pointed out in chapter 1, a mindset is a powerful thing. We don't want learners to develop a negative mindset to learning as a result of poor interactive design and technology choices. Loss of productivity and motivation are calculated along with dollars wasted. Having to correct a technology investment mistake sends shock waves throughout the enterprise. You want to do everything within your control to get it right the first time, a common theme throughout this book.

One aspect that characterizes the current state of learning technologies is continuous change. It's a moving target that includes new product offerings, new applications, new blending options, and new ideas from others. Creating a successful blend requires knowledge of the different technologies and applications available. ASTD, the leading voice of the workplace learning profession, provides a wealth of just-in-time knowledge through its website, its online newsletter *Learning Circuits,* and the many publications produced by ASTD Press. Keeping abreast of learning technologies by using these and other sources for information will not only help you keep up but also help you see how others are using technology to help learners learn. We often benefit more by seeing how to apply ideas, such as the experiences of organizations presented in these pages. The case studies accurately reflect the range of learning technologies in practice today. There are simulations, tiered learning with technology and classroom blends, the use of an LMS to track strategic learning goals, and more. With a good understanding about what learning technologies can and can't do to help you achieve the goals of the enterprise, you will be well on your way to creating the right blend.

There are many factors to consider when using learning technologies to support the success of both an enterprise strategic plan and a workforce development plan. Identifying and selecting the best options can often be overwhelming, confusing, and difficult to embed into your plan without a team voice. Your team should include those people who have a bottom-line impact on your decisions, including senior-level decision makers such as representatives from different business units and information technology (IT), the chief financial officer (CFO), representatives from HR, the chief learning officer (CLO), learners, instructional designers, trainers, and aligned vendor partners. Each organization will have a different mix of key decision makers; but whatever the mix, you need the expertise, input, and buy-in from these critical stakeholders. When you have a good understanding of the technologies available and how they can be used for strategic leverage, your conversation with decision makers will become more meaningful to them and effective for you.

It is important that you don't try to tackle learning about these technologies by yourself. To ensure that you know the needs of each operational area, engage the decision makers from those areas as soon as possible to be active members of your team.

The Needs Assessment Imperative

Having a good sense of both enterprise and learner needs, as well as current knowledge of what's available to you both internally and externally, will ensure that you have a firm foundation to decide what to use and how to make it work for you.

As with any successful learning focus, you must conduct a thorough needs assessment. Every enterprise is different, and special elements need to be embedded into the technology needs assessment. What follows is a general guide to common threads that may run through many organizations.

Learners in your organization are the targets of your learning initiatives. That may seem obvious, but it is critical to start from that understanding. They will deploy the learning content to help the organization achieve its strategic goals. A thorough assessment of learners' needs, especially as they relate to using learning technology, is a vital first step in deciding what might (or might not) work in your own organization.

A starting list of technology-targeted questions regarding learners includes the following:

- What technologies are currently available to learners?
- What differences exist in the technology available in different geographical locations?
- What training needs to be designed to help learners use technology?
- What global challenges, if any, need to be addressed?
- What are the firewall issues, if any, for your organization?
- What limitations do you have based on any of the firewall issues?
- What technologies are currently being used?
- What has worked well and why?
- What has not worked well and why not?
- What types of evaluation methods and metrics have been used or created?
- What can external partners bring to the table?
- Who is in charge of keeping up with learning technologies and applications?
- How is new information shared with key learning stakeholders?

Right now, organizations and their learning staffs are using technology in many different ways. A blended solution is a custom job. There may be common threads, such as a need for communication. Yet every organization—and perhaps even divisions—may have specialized needs. The availability of technology is the buffet on the table. What you choose should be based on sound media selection focusing on the learning objectives, the needs of the learner, the organization, and available technology.

Multigenerational Considerations

When making decisions about learning technologies, it is important to consider how to support multigenerational learners. For example, the use of learning technologies is a must in attracting and engaging learners in their 20s. Technology is the first way they learn, and they often get restless with solely instructor-led classes. In general, this group of learners is already engaged in advanced use of technology. Many of them avidly play the Internet game Second Life, where users create avatars and the environment they inhabit. They love creativity and coloring outside of the lines, as there are no lines in their minds to hold them back. Attracting and keeping these learners engaged in learning requires a great blended learning approach. Yet many organizations still have not migrated to the active, strategic use of learning technologies. Very few in this generational group ever need long-winded guidance for how to use the technology. They prefer trial and error versus looking at a manual and want information fast, now, and in small chunks.

For those on the other end of the spectrum who did not grow up with technology, including guided learning of such technology usage is a must in a strategic plan. These individuals may need more convincing that selected content can be best learned by the use of a blended approach. Many might benefit and be more comfortable with a hands-on class in how to use the technology. Many people might also benefit from technology mentors, coaches, and step-by-step guides.

Access to Technology

Where are your learners located, and what access do they have to your selected technology blend? Around the world, the answers to these questions are often different. Ensure that an access-to-technology component is included in your needs assessment, as it may vary by location. If it does vary, what can be done either to ensure that everyone is on a level field or to devise an alternate plan to make sure that everyone can participate in your learning programs? Will you prepare content that can be presented via different technology options based on the availability of technology access? You must answer questions like these to be able to support the needs of all of your learners.

Mobility

With delivery to iPods, PDAs, cell phones, and wearable technology, learning content is reaching learners who are becoming increasingly mobile. We don't stand still. Many of us travel and work in different locations. Teleworking is a popular practice that offers the same or better productivity possibilities yet is physically separated from the "real" office. "Learning to go" is a take-out option being used by those who travel extensively. With this in mind, we want to ensure that what goes into the to-go cup of learning is segmented into mobile moments.

The notion of taking classes at a central location will still have its defined place. However, with such a mobile and global workforce, technology-supported learning is not just a nice-to-have but a critical component in achieving enterprise success. Having learning content delivered through one or more technology solutions is becoming business as usual instead of an unusual way of learning. It is an important ticket to achieving success and staying competitive in the 21st century. There are many resources devoted exclusively to mobile learners, such as *mLearning: Mobile Learning and Performance in the Palm of Your Hand* by David S. Metcalf II (Metcalf 2006).

Multiple Learning Styles

The focus on learning styles is so important that I've included a chapter on this (chapter 8). Don't underestimate the power of learning styles to get learners engaged and then help them apply their new skills or knowledge. This truly has an impact on the effectiveness of your learning content and bottom line for any content design and delivery. With the use of technology, learners have increased power to be engaged—or not. If multiple styles are not addressed in the design of the content, some learners may turn off and not focus. And the hit to the bottom line can be seen in lost productivity and absence of learning content application.

There are many factors to consider in just selecting the technologies themselves (see chapter 5), and learners will decide to "turn on" or "turn off" to what's being presented based on their preferred learning style. Some learners need pictures, some love to read text and research information, some need to see demonstrations of what's been presented, and others need an audio approach throughout. Effective training should include a focus on all the different learning styles of your workforce.

The Role of the Enterprise Strategic Plan

Because instructional designers and trainers have such an impact on the bottom line, it is vital that they not only have a working knowledge of the different technologies and options available for their content design and delivery but also understand the strategic plan of the enterprise. If you took a survey of these key players on your team, how many of them would say they have read and truly understand the enterprise strategic plan? In my experience with many clients, I've found that few could describe the plan as it aligns or relates to their proposed design and delivery of the training content.

And what happens when design and delivery are outsourced? Outside vendors may not understand the enterprise strategy either, so it is critically important that key team members can translate the plan into practical guiding instructions for them. Can your instructional designers and trainers link learning to any strategic elements and best use of available technologies? Having this knowledge and educational link will serve you well when you make your case to keep your learning budget intact.

Often learners do not know about the enterprise strategic plan either. Learners tend to think about their individual needs and concerns first, with concerns about the enterprise often coming as a lower priority, if at all. Yet the enterprise has a greater chance of success if the workers are skilled and knowledgeable, which leads to increased opportunities for a better working environment, including career options. If your design and selection of learning content include deploying the material through learning technologies, first let your learners know why this will help them, and then how it will help the enterprise. If the content is linked to the strategic elements and identified, chances are that the learners will get a better picture of why this content is important both to them and the enterprise.

How Learning Technologies Can Support Your Enterprise Strategic Plan

In addition to enhancing learning, technology can play an important role in supporting the enterprise strategic plan. One of the key concepts you'll see at work in the Microsoft Xbox case study is *re-use*. Any time we can find multiple ways to use our technology framework, the cost goes down and the benefits to the enterprise increase. If we make an active, easily updated list of the strategic communication needs of those in the C suite, as well as the key business operations, we can take advantage of all technology distribution methods, not just those for dedicated learning. For example, webinars can be used for training purposes but could also be used for announcements of new markets or time-sensitive messages about change such as mergers, acquisitions, or reorganizations.

Enterprise communications is a key area where technology can support a blend of strategy and learning needs. For a fast transfer of information and knowledge, plus the ability to send a consistent message to employees, technology options to support the message and the sender are many. Technology can help deliver a consistent message, which means that people will all hear the same thing at the same time. Often, communication casualties occur when people hear different messages from different people with different spins and sometimes totally wrong information. Loss of morale and productivity and increased fuel for the rumor mill can result when strategic messages are communicated by different people. It's important to keep this in mind as you create your workforce development plan, because the implementation of strategy is often done in a mix of ways. When we can show how to use our technology-supported options for both strategic communications and learning needs, we will help to maximize effectiveness and use of our technology investments.

Another example of a learning technology–strategic win is in supporting performance efforts. Many organizations employ a balanced scorecard approach (BSC) that uses the strategies to develop effective objectives, metrics, implementation, and performance measures. The plan usually includes a strategic goal for each balanced scorecard entry. As you identify the areas listed above, it would be helpful to identify and create a communications plan that aligns with both your workforce development plan and strategic plan for the enterprise. These plans often go hand in hand. Yet we see that they don't often get linked *strategically*. And, once again, this is where technology can help support the linked goals of the enterprise from every angle.

■ ■ ■

Leveraging the Learning Advantage

- When blending learning techniques, make sure you focus on the learner.
- Blended learning content should reflect that different generations learn in different ways and that individual learners have different learning styles.
- Select learning technologies that align the content to the strategic learning needs of the enterprise.
- Learning content should be easy to distribute in the real-world lives of the learners.
- Designers and trainers should thoroughly understand the various learning technologies as they relate to learning objectives and tasks before deciding which to use.

- Selecting the appropriate technologies—and getting it right the first time—helps to attract and engage learners.
- Consider learners' access to technology when performing a needs assessment.
- Multiple learning technology solutions can address the ever-increasing need to learn on the go.
- Designers and trainers should be able to link learning to the enterprise's strategic plan.
- Learning technologies have a life beyond learning—they can also help support the enterprise strategic plan.

■■■ **4**

Blended Learning

A Strategic Application of Distributed Learning and ROI

Michael Hatt,
Former Xbox Global Training Manager,
Microsoft Corporation

Executive Summary

Real-world challenges often drive the solutions that learning professionals must implement. Time, money, resources, or even subject matter expertise are often in short supply to implement sweeping changes that are also in line with the expectations of the executive suite. This case study will demonstrate how the Microsoft and its e-learning Partner C-2 Technologies not only created a well-designed and theoretically sound learning solution, but how we built and implemented it quickly and for an extremely reasonable cost. The creative solutions presented here demonstrate one way to make your dream curriculum come true. In addition, this study will show you how to prove that training not only has value but can deliver legitimate business impact. This is a real-world example of how training (traditionally seen as a cost center versus a profit center) was able to

- implement a blended learning strategy
- demonstrate how with the right learning strategy, a one-time investment into blended learning can be used over and over to satisfy multiple business needs
- build the right pieces in the learning strategy to establish true consumption and re-use metrics around total volume of training consumed

- build the foundation for long-term ROI
- establish a best practice that may totally reshape the way training is viewed and implemented in a rapidly changing call center environment.

Finally, this case study is a testament to the committed teams working on the Xbox business, both internal Microsoft teams and external partners like C-2 Technologies.

Training Challenges of Global Outsourcing

As we begin to look into curriculum design, I want to walk you through some of the greatest challenges of working in a globally outsourced market. It is important to explain the target audience and the business model that drove this case study. As I looked at the challenges, it was particularly important to include them in the scope and pay attention to these factors. Properly addressing them was key to the successful implementation of the overall curriculum design. One thing was certain, with a target audience that is as globally dispersed as it is educationally diverse, hitting multiple learning styles and building in tracking and repeatability was going to be my team's biggest challenge.

The Business Model

I had worked as an instructional designer and project manager for training businesses in the outsource model for five years at Microsoft Corporation. Moving into the Xbox video game system world, I experienced some new challenges that I did not previously have to take into consideration as I built curriculums. If you work in a large company, you are likely to find both national and international consumers of your training. The support for the Xbox video game system operates as a global outsource model with the goal of providing the highest possible level of support for our customers in the most fiscally responsible way possible. To do this, Microsoft Corporation uses partner vendors in markets both inside and outside the United States. This enables Microsoft Corporation to find the right mix of support options for the global sales footprint of Xbox video game system products. Microsoft Corporation supports all markets the Xbox video game system is sold in with free phone support in the dominant language in that market. To effectively and efficiently reach this goal, Microsoft Corporation is a large player in the call center industry.

The business of supporting customers through call centers stirs a great deal of passion on many fronts. The political side of the call center industry should be of little concern for us as learning professionals. It is actually a great frontier where I have found the opportunity to be creative in the solutions I provide, as well as experience fascinating areas of the world. The use of the global outsourcing model for call centers is here to stay as long as the centers make financial sense and the customers who call them are satisfied with the service they receive. It is the only realistic way to give the level of customer support wanted by our consumers (free phone support) in a way that does not bankrupt the companies who provide them. This business is fascinating, and the learning challenges can be overcome with innovative design and classic educational theories. Having visited and delivered training at call centers in Canada, Egypt, Estonia, Germany, and the United States, I was able to apply the subtle differences found at each location to benefit the solutions you will see in this case study. The solutions also benefited our customers around the world by giving them a consistent experience when they needed support. In a global world, one thing is clear: No matter what you want to train, the solution needs to address as many learning styles as possible, be repeatable, updatable, and produce business intelligence on the performance of those who were trained.

The Problems

The problems (or the realities of business, as I like to call them) in Xbox are common to almost any business model. Many businesses face the same challenges in training their employees. It does not matter if they are internal assets the company hires and maintains, or external assets found through the outsourcing world, the challenges are the same. For example, retail stores face the same seasonal challenges to ramp up huge numbers of people in a short time to meet their seasonal needs. The support groups for the Xbox video game system and many other businesses have this problem. Other organizations with similar challenges are the military or the government, which have to train their people scattered throughout the world. Having worked in retail for several years and consulted with the government in my early instructional design days, I found that all experiences are good experiences and you can draw on them to solve any problems you face. As I walk you through the problems we faced in the support of the Xbox video game system, notice how these challenges can apply to any training organization.

The key business problems that our training curriculum needed to resolve were as follows:

Problem 1: Serve the multiple learning styles of a globally outsourced business.
In the global outsource world, I was faced with a target audience that spans four continents and a variety of learning styles. Additionally, for most of the target audience, English was a second language, which added another level of complexity. What was the best solution?

Problem 2: Create a program that is easy to deliver and keeps the trainers on task (in other words, is repeatable and improvable). The second major challenge I faced was to tackle the issue of not owning the resources that were assigned to deliver the training or the target audience that would receive the training. How do you motivate instructors and participants and keep them engaged in the training program when you have no direct employer/employee relationship? In this case, the target audience would be owned by the partner vendors we work with. The partner vendors also own the instructors who would train the target audience. ("Own" in this case means the partner vendors employ all their associated resources and are responsible for their staffing, performance, pay, benefits, quality execution, performance improvement, and so forth.) When faced with a model like this, the challenge is twofold:

- Getting your message to the participants in the training without interpretation.
- Getting the instructors who instruct on the vendor site to follow the curriculum as designed.

Problem 3: Design the program to account for seasonal growth in the target audience. What do you do when you have to ramp up large numbers of resources (such as in retail for various holidays) or phone support agents to support the largest product launch in entertainment history, the Halo 3 video game launch? Knowing I had to address this concern of the business while keeping the best possible mix of time in training and experience on the phones to support customers was going to be tricky. It was clear that being able to scale appropriately and create flexible curriculum paths with potentially different delivery lengths for seasonal ramping up of resources had to be a design goal. Also, re-using the standard new hire training for this needed to be a consideration to execute on the re-use goals.

Problem 4: Tracking and reporting training consumption. With a business as large and dispersed as the global support model for the Xbox video game system, how would I know that the standards and program that were designed were being consumed as they were intended? All parties wanted the numbers to show consumption as well as performance improvement and consistency. The challenge was how to get it.

Needs Analysis and Design Goals

The analysis for this project was a combination of classic needs analysis and a dash of personal experience. As I stated earlier, many businesses share common challenges. In this case, there were many that I tied to challenges faced in other areas I had worked in. It is as important for learning professionals to draw on their previous experiences in life and work to analyze and design for a specific project as it is for us to gear training toward adults bringing their experiences into the classroom. The key is that the more you can bring in outside experiences, the better rounded your solutions become. I combined retail experiences, sales experiences, previous call center experiences, and everyday observations to build the best blended learning program I could.

Analysis, the first phase of the ADDIE model (which includes analysis, design, development, implementation, and evaluation), was the first phase of this project. Having worked in the global outsource model business for several years inside Microsoft Corporation prior to joining the Xbox video game system support team, I had many ideas that I had always wanted to try. This business allowed me the opportunity to execute them. The analysis for the project began with interviews that included resources both inside Microsoft Corporation and outside with the vendor partners. After hearing from several areas of the business what they wanted if they had their dream program, it was clear that a totally new approach was needed—one that would eventually change how training was looked at in the organization.

The preliminary findings of my analysis validated the "word on the street" that changes were needed and identified additional complexities in the business I had not considered. A strong analysis will usually show that there is more to a problem than was originally thought.

The following opportunity areas were identified in the inherited curriculum:

- The curriculum needed to focus more clearly on top scenarios that an agent would face on a call.
- The curriculum as a whole needed to be scalable, and designed in a way to enable agents to grow and build skills over time.
- A fully self-paced program presents challenges for the target audience. Most of the target demographic did not learn in an exclusively self-paced environment because of diverse educational backgrounds.
- Facilitators are needed to help bridge concepts in training when they are not clear.
- A new curriculum should remove the chance for multiple interpretations of the content from both the facilitators' and participants' perspectives.
- The participants in the classes wanted more time to practice skills on the phone to acclimate properly to their jobs.
- Participants would benefit from more hands-on time with the products.

- Participants wanted more time to leverage peer interactions as a learning technique by both observing and interacting with peers.
- The program needed to provide a standardized call flow and map back to that call flow throughout the program. This is critical for a globally consistent business, as well as critical to achieve consistency in what is taught and learned. This finding ultimately began the thoughts of a global quality framework that is driven by training.
- The curriculum needed to build a clear focus on soft skills throughout. Soft skills are the interpersonal skills needed to connect with customers on the phone. This is particularly important in a global outsource model since so many cultures are interacting with cultures outside their norms.
- The electronic nature of the product and the call center environment is perfectly suited for blended learning, which would address all of the key problems found via the analysis.

One of my true delights of this analysis was the consistency of the results and the desire of all who participated to support the use a blended program. This made building the solution much easier.

The Proposed Solution (What Would Be Built)

After conducting the analysis, I had an epiphany and felt that all the stars and moons had aligned for me to create my dream curriculum. It was the same dream that others had—to build a blended learning solution, not just for the sake of pushing the technology or theory envelope in adult learning, but to give all parties involved what they wanted.

Elevator Design Goal Pitch

The design goal from the analysis was to build a workflow-based training program that blended multiple learning approaches into a cohesive learning strategy. To our stakeholders, this would show re-use, consistency, and scalability to address their wants. The strategy we were looking to build had to define a consistent assessment strategy that mapped directly to top performance indicators. The strategy would also work to establish a "recalibration cycle" for training to maintain maximum performance to a given baseline by re-using what was built for training in the quality process. The plan was to deliver to the audience a consistent message and let them know exactly what was expected of them.

The learning strategy and blended execution of that strategy needed to build a solid, repeatable, updatable, global learning solution for all our vendor partners and participants. Teaching how to achieve maximum performance for the frontline agents and addressing the ambiguity that could come from a self-paced learning approach—that was how I sold the solution as I worked out what it was going to look like. From this pitch, I formalized the project's design goals.

General Design Goals

The general design goals (or objectives) for the curriculum were to

- create strong process habits from day one
- create a truly blended learning solution
- build strong and consistent troubleshooting habits
- build strong soft skills that are repeatable and apply cross region and across businesses as best as possible
- build product expertise with hands-on experience
- create a scalable solution that builds agent skill over time
- build a curriculum that can be used to recalibrate agents to the new hire standard when their performance changes
- provide skills for tool use and build on concepts linked to the agent workflow
- provide a clear description of the frontline agent role and the boundaries of the job
- provide a structured coaching/peer learning environment to develop skills and learn from peers
- use e-learning to map to key quality indicators to be used as recalibration training and seasonal ramps.

This may seem like a lot to commit to strategically. In a nutshell, these points could be summarized as "teach the target audience how to do their job." In the strategy, you can see how the design goals are being refined to the tactical execution plan for the curriculum.

You might wonder how we came to these as the design goals. Before building this program, I was part of global support for nearly four years with Microsoft Corporation within the MSN network of Internet services business. There I saw many different approaches, traveled globally to witness support training delivered, and talked to my peers about what they had seen when doing the same. I had also listened to my stakeholders for years say, "If I had a magic wand, I would love to see…" What I found was there are key adult learning theories that always seem to apply. I also found that regardless of the business supported, everyone wanted the same thing—a consistent message that would tie to the job where we could effectively support our customers and training.

Detailed Curriculum Goals

As I moved from the general design goals to the detailed curriculum goals, at a high level I needed to stabilize the message and delivery of training to participants in the program since I was not going to be the one delivering the message directly. How would I build a program to mitigate key concerns? Here is the summary of the curriculum goals:

- **Create a truly blended delivery of content (e-learning, instructor led, and small group learning) into a single learning strategy.** I heard frequently and loudly that facilitators and participants alike wanted what all learners want—an engaging learning experience that is consistent and teaches the expectations of their jobs. The goal was to make that happen for the two different audiences, and the blended strategy was the best way to accomplish this.

- **Build scalable learning objects to address multiple business needs.** As I worked through this project, value and re-use rang loud and clear as a "have to have" throughout. When talking about this from a design perspective, I had to define what that might look like and how it could be realistically accomplished within the parameters of our business. For Xbox video game system support, this meant building learning objects that could be used by other businesses and re-used by agents and trainers alike. I also wanted to consider re-use for the quality training and recalibration of agents when they deviate from the known baseline. Without forethought into these plans, the re-use goal would not have become a reality. I also made sure to design chunks of information into small enough pieces (or nuggets, as they were called) to support the re-use goals. This allowed control of the key learning points in reconsumable training nuggets through e-learning, while allowing for facilitators to guide the program during delivery.

- **Map to key quality indicators, and provide a recalibration mechanism for quality failures.** For any business, quality monitoring, employee evaluation, and coaching are hard to make consistent in a global footprint. The Xbox case was more complicated as well since there were so many vendor partners. So how do you make this process consistent? The solution was to map the curriculum built to the key business processes or messages that the business wanted to drive. Then the business would be able to drive re-use in the quality department and deliver the exact same message when someone needed to be coached. Mapping e-learning to quality or other critical business messages and to known tools and processes used by the business ensured a sound design on all fronts.

■ **Define objective soft skills and workflow training, teaching agents how to talk to customers and work through their issues.** Knowledge is one thing, and application is altogether different. Another strategic consideration needed to be how to teach "how to do the job." I asked myself and others, "How would I want to be taught the job?" In a solely self-paced curriculum, it is up to the participants to figure out how to best do their job. This encourages a lot of inconsistency as all adult learners have different experiences and backgrounds. This leads to some pretty wide interpretations of the materials presented. So to mitigate this issue, the design had to be consistent, drive minimum interpretation, while allowing the agents to ask questions in an orderly and timely manner. Again, it also needed to focus on multiple learning styles.

Other Curriculum Goals

For the Xbox video game system support business, we had a few curriculum goals that would address business problems as well as answer a question constantly asked by our vendors: "How do you put an Xbox 360 video game and entertainment system on every desktop?" This is clearly a question that had huge financial implications for Microsoft Corporation, the Xbox video game system support business, and even larger issues for the vendor partners. The issues included possible theft, cost of TVs or monitors to support each Xbox 360 video game and entertainment system, and space in the agents' working areas for the hardware. With the want and need, we added these goals to the project design:

■ Put an Xbox 360 video game and entertainment system on every agent desk.
■ Create a software solution to put the Xbox 360 video game and entertainment system menu interface (Dashboard) on every agent desktop.

The goals seemed daunting and costly. The reality is that if you know what you want when working with the design, you can create a simple, updatable, and cost-effective solution. Ultimately, the team was able to put an Xbox 360 video game and entertainment system as well as most of the accessories you can buy for the Xbox 360 video game and entertainment system on every agent desktop through electronic 3D models. (See www.astd.org/LearningAdvantage for a link to online example of the Xbox training system.) The team was also able to provide the user interface of the Xbox 360 video game and entertainment system Dashboard on every desktop through flash animations. This shows how a daunting task can be overcome through the use of technology. These elements of design fit well into the blended strategy goals.

Project-Specific Design Requirements

The analysis showed the need to build a design that was practical and efficient—one that blended the best of what the technology world had to offer but was also scalable and maintainable for a small team of designers and developers. With all the factors that were identified in the analysis, how could this be built? Fundamentally, the solution was to break the curriculum into two key buckets:

- **Core tasks**—those that all agents need to perform on every call, and that apply to almost any support scenario. Core tasks include tools training, soft skills training, basic troubleshooting, and documentation training.
- **Line of business (LOB) tasks**—tasks and knowledge that would be specific to a line of business but still meet the scalable requirement and needs of the curriculum, while also meeting the performance needs and tasks.

Separating training tasks this way created scalable yet repeatable learning paths that complemented the blended learning goals. These focus on the mission-critical components of the business, allowing agents to grow over time while having a solid foundation as they begin their career. A military analogy to make this point would be that the agents need to come out of boot camp (or a new hire curriculum) ready to handle most key tasks and survive. They can "grow" as they learn and build good habits, as well as absorb the art of the job over time.

Fully Integrated Modular Design

When talking blended learning, we are really talking about modularity. Modularity provides options for re-use and creates the ability to have pieces small enough not to overwhelm a participant and utilitarian enough to be used in multiple ways. For example, components from the new hire program could be used for agent recalibration once they exited training. As design for this program was defined, it came together to focus on three regularly occurring training needs:

- **New hire/attrition-based training.** This training occurs as part of normal business needs for every participant who will enter the call floor. There are various types of new hire "needs" in a global rapid release business model. Drivers include increased volumes, normal attrition at call centers, or new centers coming online to support call volume or new markets.
- **Seasonal ramp up launch training.** Outside of the normal attrition and promotion-type training that vendor partners needed for participants, the business also needed "boot camp" training. This business revolves around major game releases like the Halo 3 video game, for example, or the holiday season in the United States where more consumers than normal will buy

Xbox video game system products. They may not be around the production floor long, but the participants need to be trained to the same standard in all cases.

■ **Agent recalibration back to baseline.** What do you do when a good participant's performance goes bad? When you know your audience has been taught the proper way to execute their job functions, but as time goes on they forget or pick up bad habits from others? A fully modular design will give you a third area to provide value to the business by giving a reconsumable piece of learning to get participants back to the known baseline.

Modular design in this case provided three key design benefits and especially lent itself to blended learning. The new hire curriculum allowed for a solid new hire program, a flexible seasonal training program without sacrificing agent quality, and a recalibration tool for tenured agents who built bad habits over time. A well-strategized blended learning solution will give multiple benefits while keeping with the overall design strategy.

Curriculum Design and Delivery Mix

With key strategic learning decisions made, the next consideration was the curriculum design and the delivery mix. What did we want to teach, how did we want to teach, for how long, and in what type of format? What was the curriculum to look like at a 10,000-foot-level planning for the strengths and weaknesses of the instructional mediums we were putting in the mix? Figure 4-1 shows the mix used in the solutions. To solve the problems, it was best to deliver content with the following guidelines:

■ Messages that needed to be delivered exactly as Microsoft Corporation intended were developed in interactive multimedia instruction (IMI) or e-learning.

■ Instruction that lent itself best to human interaction and those areas where an interactive dialogue would be beneficial (say soft skills training, for example) would be developed in instructor-led training (ILT).

■ Finally, a plan to let people learn from their peers. What better way to do that than to blend in small-group activities?

Blending these components (like shuffling a deck of cards) creates a curriculum that stacks the strengths of each together, while discarding the weaknesses of only using one. It also builds a strategy that is repeatable, improvable, and scalable, and addresses multiple business needs, while keeping with sound instructional methodologies.

Figure 4-1. Basic Curriculum Design

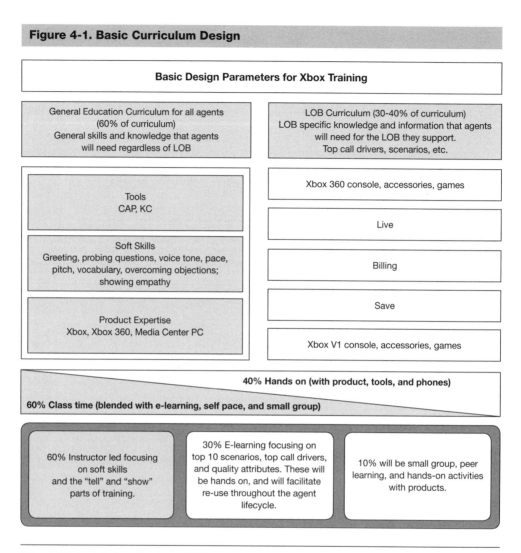

Notes: LOB stands for line of business; CAP for customer assistance portal; and KC for knowledge center.

What Would My Dream Blended Program Look Like?

This is clearly a complicated question for anyone. For me, the dream curriculum and my ideas from previous experiences needed to meet the business goals of the management team, but they also had to meet the vision. My solution used the image in figure 4-1 in the presentations when going after the financing to build the program.

The mix at the bottom of the image shows the breakdown of the different delivery mediums identified for use in the blend. The elements needed to blend seamlessly for it to be a truly blended program. Others may differ on this view and say that a blend only needs to include elements of each type. For the Xbox video game system support business, however, the blend has shown over time to be a real strength and best practice.

Another way of looking at the overall design is to look at the roles of the learning objects. The portion above the learning mix in figure 4-1 depicts the blended learning in action. The facilitator role will be to guide the learning experience. As with any new endeavor, you need a guide more in the early stages of the adventure than you do later on. You also need the facilitator to smooth out the gaps that may come from different experiences and learning styles.

The goal was to make absolutely sure that the e-learning activities used to drive the content met the participants as if the business were there delivering it. The e-learning activities also created the re-usable learning objects based on top needs identified by analysis work. This was the key to the scalable approach since the elements could be sliced and diced into different orders for different needs. Another thing to mention concerning building small e-learning activities is the smaller and more targeted they are, the easier they are to update. Regardless of how they are sliced, the business could always track and report on consumption of the training and that the key messages from the business were delivered.

The peer portion of learning allowed participants to draw on the collective group experiences. In many of our markets, participants jump from call center to call center and bring in a lot of previous experience. Using peer relationships to learn would increase the knowledge/experience level for the whole session and help to build a strong team commitment.

e-Learning Design Requirements

For the e-learning piece of the program, it is important to dig into more detail as far as design goals, and the use of IMI. In most cases, plan on e-learning to serve two purposes (remember, always think about and show how the business investment has multiple uses). As noted earlier, first it must serve new hire participants' needs. Second, it must help existing agents who need to be "recalibrated" to new hire standards. The media should be rich, interactive, and map to performance measures important to the business. Figure 4-2 shows this cycle.

As agent tenure increases, their distance from the learning event grows. As adult educators, we know that as time from the event grows, retention of the covered skills diminishes. With this in mind, how do you easily and consistently remind those with tenure how to do what they were taught? For the Xbox video game system support business, this was accomplished through our e-learning design. In an outsource model, we owned the building of materials for consumption by the

Figure 4-2. e-learning and Its Role in the Lifecycle

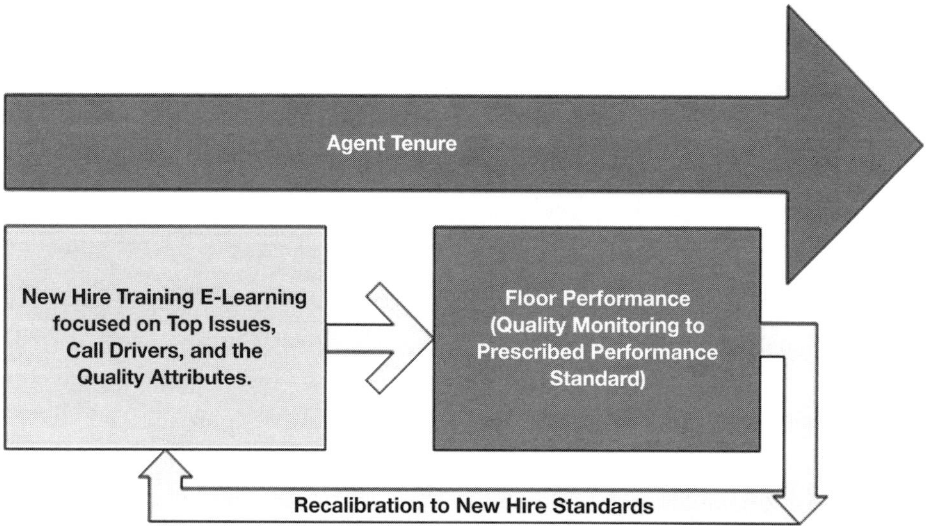

Agent Tenure

New Hire Training E-Learning focused on Top Issues, Call Drivers, and the Quality Attributes.

Floor Performance (Quality Monitoring to Prescribed Performance Standard)

Recalibration to New Hire Standards

vendor partners who support our business. However, even if we trained their facilitators, there is no guarantee they will follow the direction to the letter. Another challenge we considered using e-learning to mitigate was the mentality of "I do the job and you don't; I know more than you because you are not here and you don't know the job since you sit far away; I will do things like Frank Sinatra said, 'My way.'" We used e-learning components in our design for their strength in interactivity, structure, and the ability to repeat the message the exact same way each time they were delivered to the agents. This model created consistency in how the target audience is trained when their skills have deviated from the known baseline.

Keep in mind that the e-learning modules should be

- self-paced, media rich, and highly interactive, with the ability to be used in a blended learning environment
- designed primarily for stable topics and content to mitigate heavy maintenance needs
- focused on critical business tasks
- easy to maintain without requiring advanced coding skills, if possible
- scalable for seasonal launches
- suitable for both new hire and existing audiences
- able to refresh participants as they lose skills and need recursive training
- able to build participants' skills across multiple lines of business over time
- designed with multilingual capabilities in mind.

With this design, the program will be able to handle most common business challenges and re-use scenarios.

Now that the requirements of the e-learning components were identified, the next focus was on the ILT requirements.

Facilitator-Led Design Requirements

The traditional facilitator role will change significantly in a blended curriculum. The focus will move from someone being a purely conventional stand-up trainer who delivers the training from the front of the class to becoming a real facilitator of learning. Blended curriculums will require more from trainers in some ways. They will require that trainers be truly expert in all areas of the business they are training to effectively answer questions in the introduction and debrief portions of the curriculum. They must have the ability to lead the class seamlessly through the blend of multiple delivery methods. Given this, we had to consider our design requirements for the facilitator guides. Blended learning requires more than just reading text. It requires that facilitators be able to introduce concepts in the e-learning areas effectively, then debrief them to make sure the participants got the concept. The better executed these guides are, the more consistently delivered the program will be. For the Xbox video game system support business, we planned for the worst-case scenario when building facilitator guides. There would be times when a nontraining professional would have to pick up the program, deliver it, and not have time to prepare to teach. The individual's needs may vary and with that, so would the level of detail we would need to provide. The facilitator documentation needed to include the following:

- **Detailed facilitator notes that cover all facilitator expectations, prep work, classroom setup, and materials.** If we didn't tell facilitators specifically what to do, they would definitely do what they wanted to do. This is a must for consistency in a globally dispersed outsource model, so notes were targeted to our facilitator challenges.

- **Techniques on how to blend the multiple delivery methods seamlessly into one class**. In some cases, experienced facilitators will know this. In my experience, however, even the most hardened stand-up trainers do not have the skills and foundational knowledge to work with blended programs. They typically default to doing things their way. For example, I have seen facilitators building PowerPoint presentations to go along with our program, even though all materials are available online for participants to follow. Building a blended curriculum is as much about educating facilitators and meeting their needs as it is about building the skills of the participants.

- **Basic facilitation skills and tips**. These are often overlooked, but almost always needed. Gentle reminders are always helpful when writing facilitator materials. As long as the pointers and tips are not talking down to the audience, they should definitely be included. You never know which one might really help someone in a pinch.
- **Pre-work needed to produce product and process expertise.** This is another area where if we didn't tell facilitators what was expected, they would do what they wanted. The gap between the curriculum's expectations and the facilitators' when it comes to being prepared can be as wide as the universe is big. I have seen facilitators who are teaching programs who don't use the products, have never used the products, and don't have a desire to use the products they support. Your audience expects you to be expert at what you are talking about. How can you truly be an expert if you can't do the basics of what you are teaching? For the Xbox video game system support business, this means being good at playing at least one game. You will be challenged by your class. Many facilitators don't think about the credibility won or lost by having skills with the product being supported or the job being taught. Point this out so they remember. Tell them to do the job for a percentage of the time when they are not facilitating. Again, good reminders will help facilitators remember the little things and assist them in meeting your expectations.
- Explicitly state key learning points from the e-learning and group activities for debriefs to help facilitators blend the curriculum. If you are unclear in your facilitator materials, you can bet that your participants won't get what you want them to get out of the event.

A lot of what was covered is just good foundational instructional design. However, keep in mind how things differ from traditional ILT when you blend a curriculum and plan for it. Doing so will help guarantee that your message and that of your company gets through to the facilitators, as well as to the participants in the training.

Small Group Requirements

Group work and learning from peers are critical parts of adult learning. They are also critical parts of a well-blended learning solution. In working within an outsource model, our vendor partners have unanimously agreed that learning from peers and hands-on work are the best ways for them to learn. The e-learning and facilitator portions of the class should provide the core knowledge agents need, while the hands-on time is dedicated to practicing skills and driving the learning home. The small groups should use the knowledge they gain from the structured parts of the program to solve problems by practicing the skills they need before they reach the production floor. A primary focus should be on handling the issues and taking constructive peer feedback to build skills. I have always been amazed at how much people learn from peers and how much they enjoy doing it. As long as you can keep the environment positive, group activities are priceless learning. Plan to use them, and plan to fit them in where it makes sense in your program. There are a few areas where group activities thrive; for example, soft skills training, troubleshooting, and communication. Areas where human interaction is the focus lend themselves well to group work, where people can see, hear, and practice what they are learning in real time. In general, activities in a blended program should do the following:

- **Allow participants to be very hands on with the products.** Once training is complete, participants might not have hands-on time with products they support. They have their training and their knowledge base, but paid time to practice is often limited. Providing ample hands-on opportunities in a new hire program will help establish interest and expertise through group work.
- **Force each member of the group to present and do the activity individually, as well as in the group.** This helps participants see different views and tactics to solve the same problem, while not forcing them to be the center of the larger class.
- **Simulate the environment you are training to as best you can.** For example, if the job is a call center agent, set up activities that simulate that environment. In this example, make sure that participants can't see each other when they communicate since they won't be able to see the customer when they are on the phone. Accurately simulating the environment helps participants adopt the mindset they will need when they start the job.
- **Use group work to build knowledge of products and features to a level where participants can discuss and describe features without looking at the product.** This is key to sounding like an expert and building rapport with customers who call for support for the Xbox video game system. After all, customers expect to talk to people like themselves when they call for support. In the Xbox video game system support business, it is the expectation that gamers are supporting gamers.

One last bit of advice when blending activities into the curriculum: Use activities to bring together all parts of the program. Build off previous activities or concepts, and practice them often. The better you build this into a program, the more the participants will get the practice they need to build good habits. It is much better to do this in structured activities than to expect your audience will build them once they leave training.

Design Summary

Many factors influence the design chosen for building any curriculum. First, you need to know the audience. As discussed earlier, not only do you need to know the participant audience, but you need to know the other audience too. The two shall, and do, meet in the world of training. Use the knowledge you have of both and design for both. Facilitators and participants are equally important when considering your overall design. Design training for your audience; your design goals and reporting for the business. The two need to meet as equal partners of your blended learning solutions design to be successful on both fronts. Design and build not only for today, but for the future, and your design will be long lived and timeless, achieving the desired results.

What Blended Design Looks Like and How It Works

As discussed so far, the blend of ILT and e-learning, while not new, is open to interpretation. Part of the project was to truly blend a program. That is, alternate e-learning and a controlled message with instructor-led introductions and debriefs and small group activities to encourage peer-to-peer learning. In this section, I will introduce the overall look of each component. Then in the online demonstration, there will be a more detailed walk-through and a simulated user experience. (See www.astd.org/LearningAdvantage for a link to the online example.)

Curriculum Map

Depending on your LMS (learning management system), the map your participants should have should be simple and easy to follow. The LMS view that supported the Xbox video game system training can be seen in figures 4-3 and 4-4. This demonstrates the blend of media from the participants' view. For the curriculum, I wanted to control the flow of the course with a combination of ILT and e-learning. Each course presents the following formula:

- instructor-led introduction to the course
- instructor-led introduction to the lesson
- e-learning lesson that delivers a controlled and consistent message and pace
- instructor-led debrief of the e-learning lesson
- instructor-led debrief of the course.

The other components (such as small group activities and practical exercises) are then blended into each lesson as appropriate. This gives the course a controlled flow and provides the following benefits:

- The control, timing, and pace of the program were clearly defined.
- This format laid out a program that hit as many learning styles as possible.

Figure 4-3. e-Learning Course Map Week 1 (Participant View)

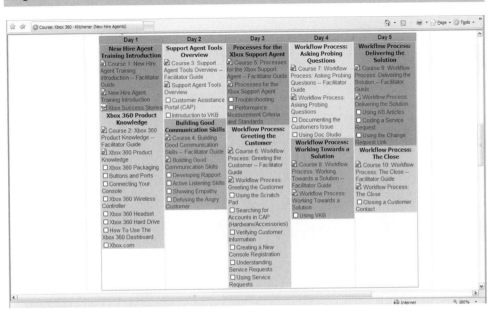

- It provided a controlled message for participants that we knew was consistent.
- The opportunity for questions and answers was provided throughout the day.
- It helped new facilitators with delivery by guiding them through the daily activities.

This format received consistent praise from both facilitators and participants alike. Each found the benefits of blended learning through application versus theory and have requested more of the same as the program evolves. I was pleasantly surprised at how well the blend works. Not only from a theoretical perspective, but the in-class results were amazing to see in action. The program created the most engaged classes I had seen in my career, while not feeling overly prescriptive to facilitator and participant alike.

Microsoft Word Documents

Design is always an area where creativity meets functionality. For the documentation facet in this program, we created a Microsoft Word word-processing software template file. The template, built with the instructional designers in mind, featured advanced form fields, auto text entries, automated icon insertion, and so on. In the e-learning portion that you can view at www.astd.org/LearningAdvantage, you will find an example. Whatever you design, be sure to push the limits of the tools you are using.

Figure 4-4. e-Learning Course Map Week 2 (Participant View)

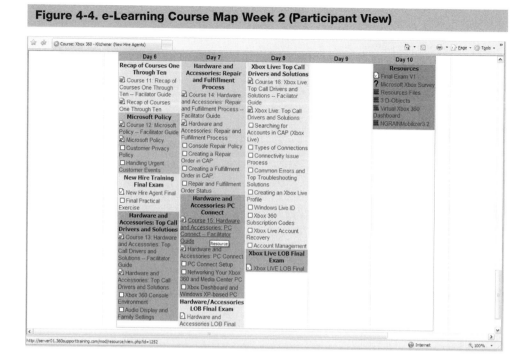

IMI Look and Feel

The design goal for the e-learning interface was to use design elements from Xbox.com and add some instructional flair to it. The design ultimately included elements from the product itself (the Xbox 360 Controller) and the colors of the Xbox 360 video game and entertainment system brand. Macromedia Flash was used to animate the "window" so the images were not static, giving it an "alive" feel. The e-learning online example provides a walk-through of the interface elements for you to use and experience. Figure 4-5 is a sample to give you an idea of the look. In this image, you can see the overall design elements and the incorporation of the 3D models into the courseware.

The online e-learning component of this book will give a great introduction and a more detailed example of how all the technologies were blended into this solution.

Evaluation and Results

Since the inception of the blended learning model in the Xbox video game system support business, there have been several key focuses:

- How can the investment achieve maximum re-use?
- How can numbers be tied to the investment?
- Can we create a model where ROI can be proven?

Figure 4-5. e-Learning Interface with 3D Model Activity

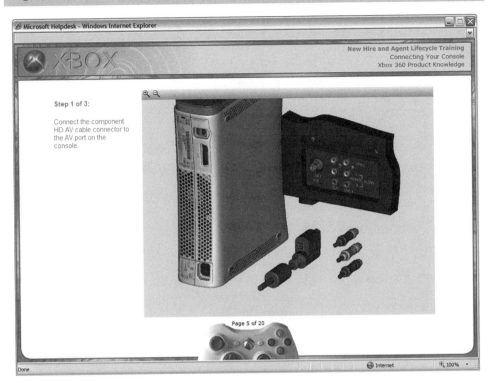

As we work through the results, I will identify where we are in our present model in blended learning and where we are poised to go. As we continue to refine and report on the results and drive our long-term, closed-loop quality framework, even the elusive ROI calculations are within reach.

The results discussed here are extremely accurate. They come from five months of work on the back-end content received from the LMS system. Using these numbers, we will help calculate estimates for the content and consumption over the last year in the Xbox video game system support business. I will not get into the details of the back-end work as it is outside of the learning area and blended learning. However, I will say that this is truly one of the most critical items to work through to effectively report your results.

Delivered Minutes of e-Learning (The Tangible Value)

This is one of the easiest areas to put up "staggering" numbers in the reporting from an LMS or through tracking delivery of your blended program. These numbers can be very exacting and sometimes difficult to gather in the views you want. As you take on building a blended learning project, be sure to consider how you intend to track and report your metrics. In my experience, where you start and where you end will be different. Each time you look at the numbers, you will find new and better ways to communicate them to the business. Here are some of the metrics we have gathered and refined as part of the Xbox video game system support business New Hire Program and other e-learning solutions.

Reduced Training Hours for All New Hires

One of the first results that we could quantify in the blended model was the estimates on time to train in the old program versus the new program. The two designs approached the same challenges differently. A cost-per-minute comparison could be used to determine long-term savings based solely on delivered minutes. This clearly shows how a blended strategy can accomplish better performance in less time, with greater re-use—the assumption in this comparison being that both programs were run by the outsource partners as designed without customization in the field.

The original Xbox video game system training program design was primarily a self-paced exploratory learning program that covered the same number of supported areas (three lines of business). It did so in approximately 115 hours of classroom training time. In addition to this, each agent trained was to go through a performance check with the trainer. This was used to prove the agent had gained all the information that he or she needed from the self-paced activities. This activity was to take approximately 8 hours per agent in the class. The new blended program implemented, for the same lines of business, 64 hours of classroom training. Assessments were included in the classroom time. Now let's look at how this program would compare to the delivered program in delivered times and costs for a set number of agents. For comparison, consider that we train approximately 8,000 agents in a given year, accounting for churn and seasonal training.

As you can see in figure 4-6, the cost in the blended learning model was less than half of the original program annually when looking at just new hire agents trained. This number is a great start. But when you consider the additional benefits of agents recalibrating to new hire after training, use for internal Microsoft Corporation employees, and additional use and benefits from other groups inside of Microsoft Corporation, the cost savings and benefits are staggering. This comparison supports how critical design is to the overall costs for different training approaches. It shows that blended learning not only costs less to deliver for comparable programs with different approaches, it is more than half as much to deliver annually. In this case study, as an intangible estimate, we can say results are showing that performance is also better when the blended program is run as designed.

Figure 4-6. Annual Cost Comparison of New Hire Programs

Annual Cost Comparison of New Hire Programs as Built for Three Lines of Business		
Variable	Original New Hire Training Program	Blended New Hire Program in this Case Study
New hire hours	123	64
Assessment time	8 hours for check outs	Included in new hire hours
Agents trained annually	8,000	8,000
Cost per hour estimate for each agent trained	$12	$12
TOTAL	$12,576,000	$6,144,000

To summarize, you can use the same content objectives, with better results, with greater re-use and cross-business benefit, and do so for half the cost annually. That, my friends, is ROI that anyone can be happy with.

Total Number of New Hire Minutes Consumed (e-learning)

In October 2006, we implemented the current blended new hire program. This program has trained over 7,000 unique users off an initial investment of $432,000. The e-learning numbers here come from one seven-month period where preparation for a major release could be captured. These numbers can be essentially doubled for a full year's worth of training in the Xbox video game system support business world. Doing this for new hires, and including the other e-learning we have developed and delivered, we have delivered (as a strong estimate) close to 1.5 million minutes of e-learning (see figure 4-7).

Total Number of Minutes Consumed (Blended)

As you can see, the e-learning minutes are impressive. But that is only part of the story. Using the numbers above and estimating for consumption of the whole curriculum (both ILT and IMI), we see that the initial $432,000 investment produced content that equaled 15,486,240 total minutes of training delivered in the new hire program since March (assuming all new users went through the eight-day new hire for the Xbox 360 video game and entertainment system and accessories only). For one year, that number would double to just shy of 31 million minutes of e-learning, which effectively shows the importance and volume of training to any

Figure 4-7. New Hire Training e-Learning Consumption Seven-Month View

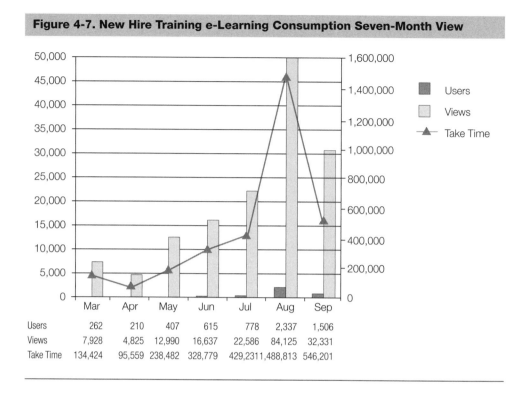

	Mar	Apr	May	Jun	Jul	Aug	Sep
Users	262	210	407	615	778	2,337	1,506
Views	7,928	4,825	12,990	16,637	22,586	84,125	32,331
Take Time	134,424	95,559	238,482	328,779	429,231	1,488,813	546,201

business owner. How does that break down for costs? The initial investment of $432,000 ÷ 31,000,000 minutes of learning = a cost to deliver of $.013 per minute.

$$\frac{\text{Project Cost: } \$432,000}{\text{Minutes of Learning Delivered: } 31,000,000} = \$.013 \text{ cost to build to time consumed}$$

Clearly, investments that show return or longevity of this type will have a significant impact on your business owners. These numbers will improve significantly as time goes on. Part of this project's long-term goal is to create a closed-loop quality framework that consistently uses new hire training for recalibration of the agents who deviate from the known baseline. This part of the project is still in its infancy, and it is too early to give exact numbers. But if used as designed, the consumption numbers could easily be doubled or tripled and the cost-per-minute delivered even smaller. This does not account for other businesses that have used and leveraged this content. Again, increasing the consumption time significantly and the cost to deliver are even further reduced.

Total Number of Minutes Consumed in e-learning for All Agents

Other parts of our blended model are to deliver new training and sustained training in an e-learning format. Figure 4-8 shows the additional training delivered in this format.

Although figure 4-8 shows the true totals of e-learning delivered as a combination of new hire and new e-learning that we launched, we delivered an additional 1,102,173 minutes of e-learning as part of our overall blended strategy. In these projects where we just build e-learning, we calculate our consumption costs per minute delivered in much the same way as a new hire program. Here, for just e-learning development divided by minutes of training consumed, we see costs in the $.06 per minute, depending on the scope of the project. Again, this is significant value in the cost to build to the number of minutes consumed.

Re-Use and Other Value to the Business (Less Tangible)

As stated throughout this case study, re-use was a key to the design of the blended learning curriculum. If you look across businesses that are similar, you can find much more re-use and additional cost savings to your company than you would think. The challenge I have when reporting results to you here is that I can only estimate their values numerically. The upside is that working across groups, establishing best practices, or sharing investments made in your space with those in other areas is not only personally rewarding, but also fiscally responsible. One day, we might be able to quantify these. For now, though, I hope the intangible or less tangible view shows you the value that blended learning can bring cross organizationally.

Figure 4-8. LMS Overall

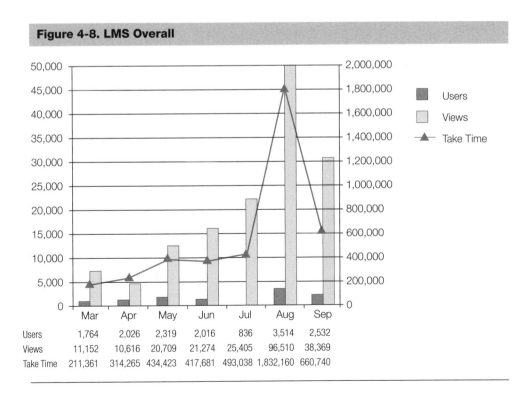

	Mar	Apr	May	Jun	Jul	Aug	Sep
Users	1,764	2,026	2,319	2,016	836	3,514	2,532
Views	11,152	10,616	20,709	21,274	25,405	96,510	38,369
Take Time	211,361	314,265	434,423	417,681	493,038	1,832,160	660,740

Does the Program Work to Deliver the Desired Business Results?

This is the multimillion-dollar question. Unfortunately, I don't have final cost/consumption/quality numbers that I can give at this time. What I can say here would fall into the intangible area with some very definitive support from the business results.

In many of our vendor partner locations, we are still working to fully implement the program and have exacting regimentation by our vendor partners. However, in a couple of instances, we have started new vendor partner locations, using facilitators approved and trained by Microsoft. The results are very promising.

When the blended new hire program is implemented, the agents are fully trained, perform higher in customer satisfaction, are better in their handle times with calls, and provide an overall better experience for our customers. As we move forward in this model, I hope to take this from the intangible column to the tangible column and give a true ROI result.

The New Product Launch

In my support division, there are several smaller groups that were able to re-use a blended learning solution that was built by the Xbox team.

Microsoft Corporation had a new project launching. It was secret, it was important, and content and information for this new business were sparse. How do you train people in this situation, especially considering the whole support model had really yet to be fully determined? How do you do this in less than a couple months and give a full blended new hire program at the same time? These are significant questions to say the least.

The solution was to use what was already built! By building a modular, blended new hire program, the team supporting this launch had most of what they needed to get started, namely a standardized workflow, soft skills training, tools training that tied to the workflow, and so on. This gave the team a real head start. This situation showed that good design can create re-use scenarios and intangible value that you can't track across multiple lines of business. The work they had to do cost less, could be done quickly, and ultimately helped them to meet difficult timelines.

Intangible value can also come as the model you build proves to be successful for your business. As we move forward in our training model, there is a very bright future for our closed-loop quality framework and agent training. But that is for another time.

■ ■ ■

Leveraging the Learning Advantage

■ The blended learning strategy created for the Xbox video game system support business uses a workflow-based training program that focuses on core tasks and line of business tasks.

■ Breaking the curriculum into two types of training tasks has resulted in scalable and repeatable learning paths.

■ Training content is delivered to the Xbox video game system support business via a mix of e-learning, instructor-led training, and small group activities.

■ When designing a curriculum, learning professionals must know their audience—both the participants and the business.

■ The blended learning model for the Xbox video game system support business has resulted in the time to train being reduced by almost 50 percent and the cost to train being reduced by more than 50 percent.

■ Creating a strong blended learning course design for the Xbox video game system support business resulted in a program that is modular and re-usable. This offers intangible value beyond the reach of what can be tracked.

■ ■ ■

Although this case study is told in the first person, it is critical to point out that an effort like this could not be done without an exceptionally strong team. I was fortunate to have such a team. Without Holland, Aaron, France, Bobby, Jeremy, Doug, Sean, the Xbox team, and our instructional design team partners and graphics artists at C2 Technologies Inc. this project could not have been accomplished.

5

Laboring Over Technology

Taking Steps to Select the Right Blend

Michael Gerwitz, e-Learning Project Manager,
U.S. Department of Labor,
and Michael Malehorn, Senior Manager,
e-Learning Infrastructure, SI International

Executive Summary

Organizations that are considering a blended learning approach to training must realize that there will not necessarily be one "best" way to accomplish blended learning. Many e-learning options exist, ranging from basic technologies—such as CD-ROMs and DVDs—to advanced technologies—for example, interactive simulations.

Organizations should also acknowledge and prepare ahead of time to address barriers to implementing blended learning. Decisions must be made about whether an organization can afford the cost of a blended learning initiative and if an organization understands how to manage the technology. In addition, the security of the networks and the capacity of the networks to handle increased data traffic must be assessed before committing to blended learning, as well as whether or not an organization's computer system needs to be updated.

No One Right Solution

The issue facing most organizations seeking to select and implement blended learning technologies today is not the technology itself; rather, it is the seemingly simple act of choosing among the technologies available.

Senior-level managers responsible for selecting and implementing myriad e-learning technologies are often faced with a set of opposing constraints when it comes to technology and organizational requirements. There is usually no one single answer—no one "right" or "best" or "optimal" technology that solves every set of requirements for every organization. Rather, the method for selecting the right technology to support an organization's blended learning needs involves understanding multiple issues and then selecting the solution that represents the best fit between the organization's needs and the various competing constraints of infrastructure, budget, and change management.

Barriers When Choosing Blended Learning Technologies

Blended learning technology has sufficiently advanced in terms of capability to support almost every training need imaginable. We currently can

- create and distribute animations that teach and demonstrate complex mental models, and use them to augment or complement an instructor in a classroom setting, as well as deliver that animation as part of an online course via a learning management system (LMS)
- leverage Internet technology to provide fully interactive, live, instructor-led sessions to remote or geographically dispersed learners. These provide learners much of the same opportunities to interact with instructors, ask questions, and seek clarification and insight as do traditional classroom sessions.

The limitations related to selecting and implementing blended learning technologies are no longer ones of the technologies being unable to support the learning required; rather, we are now facing limitations placed by the organization itself. In the past, we often found ourselves wishing we could deliver live, instructor-led sessions to remote locations. Today, we can do this through a variety of software and hardware combinations. So now, instead of wishing we had the technology, we find ourselves wishing that we could actually implement it within our organization. The limiting factor to widespread adoption and use of blended learning is not the lack of technology. It is the lack of organizational capability to select, implement, and effectively use the technology. Organizations face roadblocks related to the computer capabilities of their learners; networks that can't handle the high-data transmission requirements that some blended learning technologies demand; or insufficient funds to purchase, install, and maintain the technologies within their existing budgets. Often, full implementation of blended learning within an organization is not prevented by shortcomings of technology, but by shortcomings of infrastructure and budget.

This is not to say that these shortcomings can't be overcome. But individuals must take the shortcomings into account when they decide they want to leverage these technologies to address the needs of their learner population. They can't simply buy something and expect it to work in their organization. They must plan, create requirements, and evaluate the organization's ability to use and support the technologies well before they focus on a solution. Identifying these organizational issues ahead of time will not only help in selecting the technology with the best fit for an organization, it will help in avoiding the costly mistakes of purchasing something that can't be used.

The purpose of this chapter is to help explain the various issues that may have to be addressed when individuals attempt to use blended learning technologies in their organizations so they can be better prepared to make informed decisions. We will now discuss the various technologies available and paint a general picture of how these technologies are used.

The Relationship Among Technologies

The simplest way to understand the current state of blended learning, without getting into a highly detailed discussion of the technologies themselves, is to think about where these technologies fall in relationship to one another. Picture a straight line that represents the current state of these technologies with the two endpoints defined in terms of how these technologies are used in conjunction with each other. On one end, technology is used to present electronic material within a classroom environment. This material would be peppered in traditional, instructor-led classroom sessions as animations, movies, or images to increase student comprehension and retention. This is the classic example of the modern "electronic classroom" that we see in high schools, colleges, and corporate and government facilities now. At the other end of the spectrum, Internet/network technologies are leveraged to distribute live, self-paced, web-based, or virtual classroom sessions through an LMS to a geographically dispersed audience. This approach represents how most large government and corporate organizations provide learning to their employees.

The midpoint of this line is what most organizations typically implement as a "blended learning" approach. This represents a combination of classroom-based sessions at a discrete location (such as a formal training facility or classroom) with online material that is delivered to students remotely via network or Internet connection.

Factors That Create Difficulties

As mentioned earlier, the biggest issue affecting organizations when implementing blended learning technologies is not typically the technology itself; rather, it is a combination of factors internal to the organization that creates the most difficulties. Some typical examples are

- inflexible information technology (IT) and computer security policies
- outdated or inadequate investment in computer network capabilities
- lack of financial planning to account for maintaining computer capabilities within the organization, including the costs of acquiring and implementing these technologies into the organization
- user adoption, usually represented by a lack of computer literacy.

However, these issues are not impossible to overcome. Their existence must be recognized, and the organization must address them up front and realize that if it is to truly achieve the benefits of blended learning, some changes will need to be made.

Types of Learning Technologies

The learning technologies currently being used are as follows:

- Basic
  - Instant messaging (IM) software
  - Telephone/teleconferencing
  - Video
  - CD-ROM
  - DVD
  - Movies/animations via computer
- Intermediate
  - LMS
  - Online content (webpages, collaboration tools, discussion forums, web-based training)
- Advanced
  - Interactive simulation (practice systems, interactive avatars, games)
  - Virtual instructor sessions delivered via web
  - Adaptive content (context sensitive material)
  - Expert systems (interactive coaching tools, performance support).

Some of these technologies—such as teleconferencing, CD-ROMs, and animations—are familiar to many people, while others—such as LMS and interactive simulations—are only just now starting to become more commonplace in the learning environment. Each has a place in the blended learning landscape; however, not all of them are necessarily applicable to an organization's needs. The trick is to determine the best mix or "fit" of these technologies for an organization's goals, budget, and technical environment. The focus of the following discussions of these technologies will not be on the technical end, but on the simple pros and cons related to these categories as a whole.

Basic Technologies

Basic technologies are familiar to most learners, if not computer users in general. These are technologies that are commonplace in both an office and home computer environment. We can purchase home computers that create either CD-ROMs—or CDs, as we refer to them—as well as DVDs. We use them to store documents, pictures, or music and to send these files to other people. As a frame of reference, in the e-learning community only 10 years ago this technology was so expensive that only organizations dedicated to developing distributed e-learning could afford to invest in it. Now, it's not possible to purchase even a simple low-cost computer without it.

This is a powerful point to keep in mind when examining how to connect blended learning with learners. The pervasiveness of these basic technologies today offers a simple and effective way to reach learners with a minimal investment in technology by the organization or the learners.

The downside to these basic technologies is that they are difficult to combine together into a single approach that makes life easy for the learner. These technologies tend to be single programs or items that require coordination with the learner or, for detailed instructions, are delivered to learners before they engage in the learning event. As an example, it is possible to have learners available through a teleconference or IM session while they work their way through an interactive training course that was sent to them on a CD. However, to ensure that learners understand what they need to do to participate, they must be told what to do, when to do it, and what their expectations should be. This can be difficult to coordinate and can also limit the times when this type of coordinated learning approach can be accomplished. So the overall drawback to these basic technologies is that they are not easy to combine into a single approach to reaching learners. They are typically better used in single elements of a larger learner intervention, such as a CD that learners can use as stand-alone, self-paced training, followed later by a teleconference or IM session to address questions learners may have afterward.

Here are some questions to think about when looking at basic technologies:

- Are my learners geographically dispersed?
- Does my material change often?
- Does my audience access training at specific times, like during business hours, or do they access training mostly from home?
- Do I have the staff to create CDs and mail them to my learners?

Intermediate Technologies

Intermediate technologies are typically part of an organizational approach to disseminating learning to an audience. The costs associated with acquiring and implementing these technologies can be quite high—on the order of tens or hundreds of thousands of dollars, depending on the size and scope of the technology being used. As an example, a recent LMS implementation project within a large government agency is planned to span four years and cost $500,000 for the software, hosting, and implementation services just to get the project running.

Such an example should not scare anyone away from these types of technologies. Rather, it should serve as a starting point for planning and budget discussions with an organization. The general rule of thumb for these types of technologies is the more capabilities the software or technology has, the more expensive and time consuming it will be to implement. At the low end of this cost scale are webpages and online content. The basic technology for online content is familiar to anyone who has surfed the Internet or web, requiring an investment in a web server to store and deliver the pages, and a package or "authoring tool" to create the pages. Examples of simple authoring tools for creating web pages would be Dreamweaver or FrontPage. To reduce the cost of putting material online, an organization can pay a company to store or "host" its content rather than purchase its own servers, routers, and so forth. This reduces maintenance requirements for this technology since under this type of arrangement an organization is also paying the hosting company to maintain its equipment.

The advantage of this type of technology is that it leverages the Internet to deliver training to learners from a single location. The term *deliver* is somewhat misleading since the content that learners will use is actually in a single location. Rather, they are accessing the information from one source. Having one location for learners to access content not only reduces an organization's costs for updating the material, but also helps to ensure that out-of-date information does not confuse learners. Contrast this with the use of CDs, which cannot be updated to reflect changes in information. In the CD approach, to update the information on each CD, discs would need to be sent to each and every learner affected. This problem does not exist for web-based delivery technology, since all material can be sent to learners from a single location.

Moving further into this type of technology, we reach the category of "online content," which just means that the instructional material has more Internet technology embedded in it. Most people are familiar with web-based training (WBT). This is just an example of one type of online content. Other forms can include technologies that allow for more real-time interaction with instructors or other students, facilitate question-and-answer sessions, or permit the sharing of knowledge among learners. Unlike basic technologies, where it is difficult to combine the various interactive tools together into a single event, this type of technical approach allows these tools to be combined to provide a more immersive learning environment.

Through an LMS, an online course can be created that comprises a WBT event and an online discussion or question-and-answer session through a discussion forum within the system. This is the border of the typical definition of blended learning, where we begin to combine multiple instructional strategies to improve knowledge transfer and knowledge retention on the part of the learner. This also begins to replicate the type of supportive learning environment that people tend to be familiar with in the guise of formal school and university environments.

It is clear that these intermediate technologies have some tremendous pros behind them, which is why they are becoming more commonplace in large-scale learning strategies for organizations, businesses, and government. But, as with everything in life, there is no free lunch. We've already touched on one of the cons associated with this type of technology—the costs. While it is possible to get LMS software for little or no cost through the use of open-source software, there are still the costs associated with implementing the technology into an organization's environment. This is the other big downside to this technology—the costs associated with updating or changing an organization's computer infrastructure to leverage it.

Infrastructure is simply the basic facilities, services, and installations supporting the computers and networks in an organization. Individuals should research what makes a computer or Internet network operate before getting too far into promoting this technology in their organization, since this is the actual path that learners will take to reach the material on either the organization's server or the LMS. Simply put, the best instructional approach and content in the world is of no value if learners can't reach it due to computer or network problems. So, the con here is that an organization's existing technical capabilities can have a significant negative impact on its ability to implement this intermediate level of technology.

Here are some questions to think about when looking at intermediate technologies:

- Are my learners geographically dispersed?
- Does my material change often?
- Do I need or want to track the progress of my learners through courses?
- Do I have the staff available to support Internet and network systems?
- What are the capabilities of my organization's computer systems and networks?

Advanced Technologies

Advanced technologies allow almost anything in a learning program to be done remotely. These technologies reflect the Holy Grail of e-learning: being able to address any training requirement or teach any subject or skill through electronic means. To put it in perspective, over a decade ago, the technology roadmap for a large U.S. government department identified a target of training technology for 2010 to be the "holodeck," referring to the fully immersive environment depicted on the *Star Trek* series on TV at the time.

While we still have a long way to go before achieving that type of capability, there are technologies available today that even 10 years ago didn't exist outside of some U.S. Department of Defense research and development environments. One example is the ability to create highly accurate simulations that can be sent over the Internet to teach high-level decision making. A real-world application is the use of interactive simulations to aid in diagnosing and troubleshooting electronic systems in the airline and telecommunication industries. Only 15 years ago, these types of simulations existed solely in the realm of the military due to the high costs of creating the material digitally, then combining it with the high data-rate networks needed to send it to the students.

Now, this technology has matured to the point where the costs are no longer discussed in terms of millions of dollars, but rather less than half that amount. Granted, it still takes a set of highly skilled individuals to create instructional material that effectively uses this type of technology, but these individuals are now easier to find than a decade ago.

Even on a simple level, one can conduct synchronous or "live" training sessions between an instructor and students who are geographically separated. This technology was also solely in the realm of the military just a decade ago. Or consider the web conferencing capabilities that exist now, and, in some businesses, are a daily way of life. This technology, while it existed 10 years ago, was so cost-prohibitive that few organizations outside the federal government could afford to acquire it. Now, however, it is readily available.

The advantages of this type of technology are well documented—it is the pinnacle of the blended learning approach in that it allows the organization to address any requirement its learners may have. When applying context-sensitive training, material and delivery mechanisms can be created that adapt to the specific needs of the learner at a particular moment in time. An example would an electrical wiring diagram for a complex system that could be used as orientation training for one set of learners, but when bundled in a context-sensitive application, could show a user only the specific sections of the diagram that are relevant to troubleshooting a problem on the job. This information could even be reformatted to display on a technician's PDA or tablet PC, depending on the need.

As might be assumed, the biggest con associated with this type of technology is the cost, both of the technology itself and the software needed to develop the content in the first place, as well as the infrastructure needed to deliver it. An example of the infrastructure issue is highlighted by the scenario given in the preceding paragraph, which assumes that the technician has either a PDA or tablet PC to use in the field as a job aid. If he or she doesn't, then this delivery mechanism may not be cost-effective.

In addition, there is a staffing disadvantage associated with this level of technology; the skills that the developers and designers must have to create the material itself typically lead to higher salary requirements for them than for individuals involved with other technologies. Consider the technical skills needed by a graphic artist when creating animations compared to static images. This cost is often overlooked when organizations begin to integrate this type of technology into their learning strategies. Yet it is a critical cost. The quality of the instruction delivered depends greatly on the skills of the people who are designing and developing it. This fact doesn't change just because it is becoming easier to develop the material.

Here are some questions to think about when looking at advanced technologies:

- Do my learners have complex learning or knowledge requirements?
- Does my material apply to multiple presentation methods?
- Is my material complex enough to require simulation or approaches that adapt to user input?
- What are the capabilities of my organization's computer systems and networks?
- Can I afford the software and staff needed to develop the material in the first place?

Limitations That Can Impact Implementing Blended Learning Technology

Limitations affecting the adoption and implementation of blended learning technologies tend to revolve around two main points: organizational and technical.

Organizational limitations:

- **Budget**—Can the organization afford to purchase the technology (software, licenses, and hardware)? Can it afford to install the technology, maintain it, and keep it running to support the learners within the organization?
- **Policy**—Does the organization understand how to manage how the technology is used, how it is provided to the learners, how to determine if it is effective, and how to determine what gets delivered to whom and when?
- **Management**—Does the organization's management understand how the technology can be used to support the needs of the learners? Do they support the use of the technology? Do they understand the limitations of the technology?

Technical limitations:

- **Network security**—Does the technology make the organization vulnerable to unauthorized access (hacking) by users outside the organization? Does the technology allow users to provide information deemed sensitive to the organization to an external party? (Example: Information sent via IM is claimed to be the property of the company, which created the IM program itself.)
- **Network speed**—Does the organization's network have the ability to support the increased data traffic the technology may add while still handling the normal data traffic necessary to support daily work processes? This is typically referred to as "bandwidth." Implementing some blended learning technologies can add so much extra traffic to the network that the network slows to the point where functions critical to everyday work (such as email and accessing network storage drives) fail to respond, or the network itself crashes.
- **Hardware**—Can the organization's computer systems use the technology? In some cases, the technology cannot be used in the organization until the operating system of every user's computer is updated or replaced with a newer version that can support the technology required. A simple example would be the need to update a user's browser version (from IE 5.5 to IE 6, for instance) to use the latest version of Macromedia Flash. While this appears to be a simple

update/upgrade for a single system, it becomes more complicated and cost-prohibitive as the size of the organization increases. Simply put, it takes more people and more time to update the computers of a large organization than it does for a small one, assuming the organization has the staff available to perform the update.

Some of these points have already been alluded to in this chapter. There are ways to overcome or address these limitations, if individuals are willing to do three things. First, experts within the organization should be asked for their input, guidance, and assistance. No single person has to be the expert on all these subjects, but someone has to be able to ask the right questions of the people who are. Second, individuals creating a blended learning strategy should realize that the best way to address these limitations is to examine them well in advance of creating the strategy. The strategy should not be created first with the expectation that these challenges will be addressed later. Some of these issues, such as cost or infrastructure, can only be resolved by up-front planning and budgeting. And, third, there must be a willingness to accept that one or more of these issues may not be able to be resolved, which thus requires a willingness to adapt a plan to accommodate the limitations of the organization. While these three dicta seem to be common sense, it's typically what we take for granted as "common sense" that dooms the best intention and strategy.

The best approach to these three dicta is to research both the organization and the various technologies that would ideally be implemented. The skills and technical know-how of not just the development staff, but also the learners should be examined. Do they have the skills required to leverage advanced simulations? Do they have the Internet or computer capabilities to leverage them? If learners are waiting two or three minutes for a simulation to download over their dial-up Internet account, chances are they won't have a satisfying learning experience. Conversely, while learners may have the capability to use the most advanced technology available, does the content require it? If the bulk of the content can be addressed through static images or instructor-led slides, the question to ask is if more advanced technology is really needed.

The bottom line is that while technology can help address human performance shortcomings, technology is *not* always the best solution to addressing them. No one should become so enamored with the technology that he or she loses sight of the fact that the whole purpose of a blended learning plan is to address some requirement that learners have that the current plan can't address.

Here are some suggestions for connecting the distribution channels for learning to a learning plan:

- The issue facing most organizations is not how to connect the distribution channels into their learning plan. It is making sound decisions that effectively scope out the type of technologies to be used and how to address the various impacts the technology will have on the organization (picking the right technology for a learning plan). The biggest mistake most organizations make is assuming they can "add," "retrofit," or "insert" blended learning technology to their existing learning plan without going back and examining the plan to see if it can support the addition of the technology in the first place.
- To determine the right blended learning technology for an organization's training plan, consideration must be given to the various limitations identified above. Here are questions to ask:
  - How much can I afford to spend on the technology?
  - Do my learners (or does my organization) have the ability to use the technology on the current computers?
  - Does the organization have the staff available to support user questions when they encounter difficulties in using the new technology, and are the users savvy enough to be able to understand the technology and how to use it?

One of the emerging challenges related to integrating new technology into organizations is associated with migrating both data and existing content from a current system to a new one. This can be due to the adoption of different standards, the limitations of the older technology, or any number of other reasons. However, the critical point that any organization must understand is that it is much better off identifying those issues up front when adopting or implementing newer technologies than attempting to address them afterward.

■ ■ ■

Leveraging the Learning Advantage

- There is usually no single learning technology that will address all of an organization's needs.
- The computer skills of the learners, limited networks, and insufficient funds can hinder the use of blended learning. Careful planning can help overcome these roadblocks.
- Basic learning technologies, such as CD-ROMs and DVDs, are inexpensive but difficult to combine into a single approach.

- Intermediate technologies, such as learning management systems and webpages, use the Internet to deliver training to learners from a single location and are easy to update; however, they can be costly to implement.
- Advanced technologies, such as interactive simulations, allow organizations to address any of their learners needs, but they are expensive in terms of infrastructure and staffing.
- Technology is not always the only answer when it comes to addressing human performance shortcomings.

6

Managing Learning to Ensure Strategic Alignment with the Business

Fred Goh,
Former Director of Strategic Learning,
Caterpillar University

Executive Summary

One of the greatest challenges of managing training is partnering with the entire business enterprise to ensure alignment, commitment, support, and results. Because of the global nature and decentralized culture of Caterpillar, addressing this challenge was a daunting task. Given that the company has over 94,000 employees organized into 30 business units spread out in more than 70 countries, creating a consistent annual process to assess learning needs and identify the high-impact learning initiatives to meet these needs was a complex task.

However, while the complexity of the situation was a challenge, it also presented an opportunity. There existed the potential of annual savings through centralization. Centralizing and making the needs assessment and learning planning process more strategic offered the further promise of delivering learning that was not only more efficient but also more effective with a higher return-on-investment (ROI) for the business.

The Enterprise Learning Plan (ELP) process was designed and deployed as a companywide practice to assess the learning needs of each business unit and plan learning for the entire business enterprise. The success of this process has enabled the ELP to evolve and grow into a powerful standard business practice.

About This Case Study

Caterpillar University and former Director of Strategic Learning Fred Goh have received numerous awards for their excellence in learning. ASTD's BEST and Excellence in Practice Awards have been bestowed on this *Fortune* 100 organization. Why reinvent the wheel to keep your training budget intact when the road has already been paved for you? Every organization is different. Yet the common-thread steps contained in this case study can be used as a benchmarking model and checklist for your own plan. Creating an environment where strategic benefits are clearly seen through strategic learning initiatives is the desired end result. The impact on the enterprise to provide funding is a must. This case study is an excellent example of this principle.

With learning closely tied to business strategies and processes, Caterpillar's learning budget over the past few years has been steadily growing during challenging business scenarios.

One unique feature of this process is the inclusion of an evaluation strategy that guides evaluation and ROI studies and tracks benefits. ROI studies have shown that over $160 million in annualized benefits to the business have been delivered over a six-year period.

Strategic Planning for Learning and Development at Caterpillar

Caterpillar University was created in 2001 to provide leadership for enterprise learning and to ensure that the company has the intellectual capital to succeed in an increasingly challenging environment. The university's mission is to improve the performance of company employees, suppliers, dealers, and customers. Central to this mission was introducing an enterprisewide process that enabled strategic decisions about learning to be made so that resources could focus on learning with the greatest strategic value and business impact.

The original goals of this process—the ELP—have not changed since its inception. It has evolved and grown as a standard business practice. When this process was launched, learning leaders of each business unit (25 at the time) focused more on simply taking inventory of learning programs and informally deciding on priorities. Initially, input from business unit leaders was minimal. Today, however, business unit leaders are fully engaged in planning for learning on an annual basis in line with their business strategies. Recently, the department heads (one level down from business unit leaders) have also been engaged in strategic learning planning.

The ELP is centrally administered by the corporate university to 30 business units operating in over 100 facilities in more than 70 countries. This practice ultimately serves over 94,000 employees. In addition, more than 90,000 dealer employees are served, as well as suppliers and customers.

Resources and Commitment to Ensure Successful Implementation

In addition, the university's president, five deans, and two functional managers spend in total about 40 days per year on the ELP ($28,000). Business unit learning leaders each spend about 20 days per year on the process ($250,000), and business unit leaders and department heads each spend about one day per year ($70,000). In addition, there is about $20,000 in associated materials and travel costs for a total annual investment of about $368,000. The lifetime cost (based on three years) is about $1.1 million.

What Sets This Practice Apart from Other Similar Practices?

The ELP is differentiated from other needs assessment/learning planning practices according to the following features (see figure 6-1):

- **A high level of partnership between learning leaders and business unit leaders, especially in a highly decentralized business culture.** The decentralized nature of the company went against the grain of a centralized unit that could in a sense "dictate" to the business units what learning they would initiate and when. The key to success was partnership. Caterpillar University had to be—and be perceived as—a valued partner delivering strategic learning initiatives, and not a corporate group dictating learning to the business units. The unique and highly structured design of this process focused learning and business leaders only on those most strategic learning needs that provided a strong foundation for partnership. The logic of a centralized process became readily apparent as the perceived learning needs across the enterprise were viewed as common and shared. Common needs can be met with common learning initiatives. Partnering across the business units was viewed as essential to leverage assets and learning that best met the strategic learning needs.
- **A focus on driving the strategic outlook of learning, and not just a year-to-year planning exercise.** The ELP process explores and expands senior leader expectations for how learning will enable the achievement of business goals. The ELP conversations that learning leaders have with business leaders explored learning and business needs over a three- to five-year period of time.

Figure 6-1. Organization of Learning and Governance

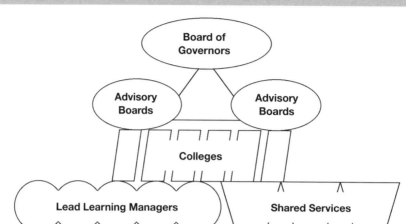

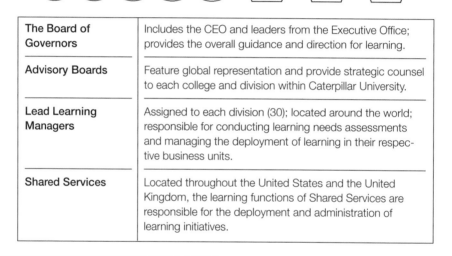

The Board of Governors	Includes the CEO and leaders from the Executive Office; provides the overall guidance and direction for learning.
Advisory Boards	Feature global representation and provide strategic counsel to each college and division within Caterpillar University.
Lead Learning Managers	Assigned to each division (30); located around the world; responsible for conducting learning needs assessments and managing the deployment of learning in their respective business units.
Shared Services	Located throughout the United States and the United Kingdom, the learning functions of Shared Services are responsible for the deployment and administration of learning initiatives.

- **A vast scope, breadth, and global reach.** The end-use audience for this process represents nearly 190,000 learners (including both employees and dealer employees) in more than 70 countries speaking 12 major languages.
- **A powerful metrics and evaluation component that drives accountability for results and demonstrable business impact.** The evaluation strategy was a key component of the ELP. This strategy outlines how each of the ELP learning initiatives will be evaluated according to the Kirkpatrick/Phillips five levels of evaluation. The evaluation strategy is periodically reviewed and updated. ROI studies are done on selected initiatives, the business impact is evaluated in terms of the learning initiative goals, and recommendations are

made to increase the business impact of the initiative. The results from all completed ROI studies are organized into a summary document that captures the ongoing value-add of learning to the business. To date, ROI studies have documented that over $160 million of annualized benefits have been delivered to the business from 2002 through 2007.

Proposed Solution and Goals

Soon after Caterpillar University was established, senior leaders expected answers to their questions about the value that learning was adding to the business. Over $100 million a year was being invested in learning, and leaders wanted to know that this investment was being made in the learning initiatives that were most strategically critical for the business.

As Caterpillar University took shape and all learning initiatives were examined, it was clear that there were many opportunities to improve how learning was planned and managed. Among the 30 business units spread around the world, there were many examples of duplicative learning initiatives. Different business units designed and developed learning initiatives that were essentially the same. Gaps in learning curricula were also observed. For example, there were insufficient learning offerings for frontline supervisors. Plus there was a lack of consistency across the business enterprise. Some business units provided rich learning environments; while for other business units, learning opportunities were sparse.

Caterpillar University, in full partnership and support from its board of governors, documented the need for a common, consistent process to conduct a strategic learning needs assessment upon which to base investment decisions. The board, consisting of the CEO and several of his direct reports, understood the business value of designing and using this strategic learning needs assessment, as well as the costs of not doing so. Millions of dollars were being siphoned from strategic learning investments through duplication and waste.

Caterpillar University facilitated a comprehensive needs assessment to best design this new approach to enterprise learning planning. Business unit leaders and learning leaders from around the world participated in documenting learning management and spending practices. These activities not only contributed to pinpointing root cause issues with the current learning planning processes but also enabled business and learning leaders to embrace the need for change. The status quo was no longer acceptable. The new question was how best to design an enterprise learning planning process.

Designing the Enterprise Learning Plan

Caterpillar University's board of governors ultimately made the decision to deploy the ELP process based on the design recommended by Caterpillar University. The board's decision was supported by the business unit leaders and learning leaders who would deploy and use the process. The design of the ELP appropriately addressed the following issues:

- **Consistency.** The process applied to all appropriate business units and was well documented and communicated. Training sessions were conducted so that business and learning leaders throughout the enterprise acquired the requisite knowledge and skills to execute the process consistently and effectively.
- **Leadership engagement.** All leaders were consulted early in the learning planning process regarding their business strategy and needs, and how learning could meet these needs. Each business unit leader partnered with learning leaders and Caterpillar University to develop their division learning plans.
- **Business focus.** The key determinate that influenced the investment decisions for learning initiatives was business need. Learning initiatives were specifically linked to business critical success factors. Initiatives with relatively weak links to the business critical success factors were not invested in.
- **Customer focus.** The business enterprise was viewed as including customers, dealers, and suppliers, as well as employees. Enterprisewide learning initiatives were expected to have a positive impact on this broad set of learners—either directly or indirectly. Some learning, for example, directly includes customers, while other learning initiatives indirectly had an impact on customers through dealers or other groups.
- **Integration.** Enterprise learning planning is integrated with other appropriate people-related planning processes, such as individual development planning and succession planning.
- **Results orientation.** A rigorous evaluation process was put in place to ensure that the process was well managed, continuously improved, and delivered the expected results to the business.

The ELP has successfully addressed the performance issues of inconsistent execution of learning planning that led to inefficiencies and that underserved the business. It enabled Caterpillar to identify common learning needs and execute shared learning initiatives. For example, many business units were on the verge of developing their version of change management training. Using the ELP, Caterpillar identified common change management needs for the enterprise, adopted a change management methodology, and developed a common learning initiative that was shared by the business units.

Alignment

The ELP has had a powerful influence on integrating learning with other people-related planning processes and with aligning learning to business goals. Employees design their individual development plans in consultation with their managers. Learning opportunities are selected from curricula, which are designed based on decisions made during the annual ELP process. The ELP decisions reflect business leader input and expectations, as well as direct links to business goals (for example, critical success factors). In this way, the ELP ensures alignment from business goals to the learning of individual employees.

The ELP is also integrated with the leader supply process, which includes succession planning. All leaders above a certain level have career path options that are spelled out. Expectations for timing and readiness are also identified. The ELP reflects the learning needs of these leaders and provides them with the learning opportunities to accelerate their readiness for new challenges and their ability to exercise their career path options.

Caterpillar University followed the ELP to align learning to business goals and outcomes:

- Conducting one-on-one interviews with each member of the board of governors and the executive office
- Analyzing data to identify common themes and business issues for the next three to five years
- Gleaning strategic learning needs from the themes and issues
- Reviewing a summary of the business issues and learning needs with the business leaders to gain their understanding and buy-in.

The ELP process is designed in a step-by-step fashion to drive the alignment of learning to business goals (see figures 6-2 and 6-3). Caterpillar University consolidated the 30 division learning plans submitted by the division learning managers. Then Caterpillar University and the appropriate advisory boards evaluated the learning needs and initiatives. They grouped common learning needs together and consolidated learning initiatives. They also identified top learning initiatives and linked each to the corporate strategy. By doing so, Caterpillar University and the advisory boards established a clear line of sight from the needs of individual business units to the needs of the corporate business enterprise (see figure 6-4).

ELP Process Exemplifies Partnership

Caterpillar's 30 divisions each develop their annual learning plan in partnership with Caterpillar University. These learning plans are based on enterprise learning needs,

Figure 6-2. Aligning Learning to Business Goals through the ELP Process

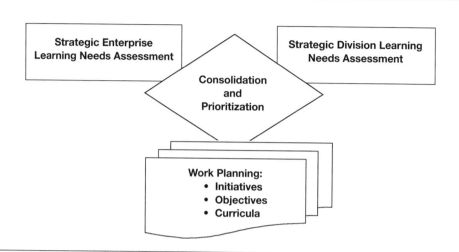

which Caterpillar University compiles, as well as each division's own organizational learning needs. The learning needs assessment process ensures that the business leaders and learning leaders follow a highly collaborative process. Senior executives, business managers, learning leaders, Caterpillar University management, and others are all brought into the final selection of strategic learning initiatives.

Given that the strategic learning initiatives also cover marketing and sales, this process goes beyond employees to include dealers, suppliers, and customers. Caterpillar business managers and learning leaders partner with the dealers to understand and meet their learning needs. For example, College of Marketing and Distribution partnered with dealers and designed a comprehensive competency-based needs assessment and curricula for the dealer employees.

The ELP process also highlights gaps in the learning community's capability to design and/or deliver certain kinds of learning. Partnerships are formed with external suppliers to fill in these gaps. For example, when the ELP highlighted gaps in senior leader learning opportunities, the College of Leadership partnered with a university to provide content for a leadership development program.

Safety provides another example. Caterpillar has established safety as a business priority; therefore, safety learning was established as an ELP priority. The College of Technology then partnered with the global safety process owner as well as internal and external safety-training providers to design and deliver a comprehensive safety curriculum.

Figure 6-3. Strategic Division and Enterprise Learning Needs-Analysis Process

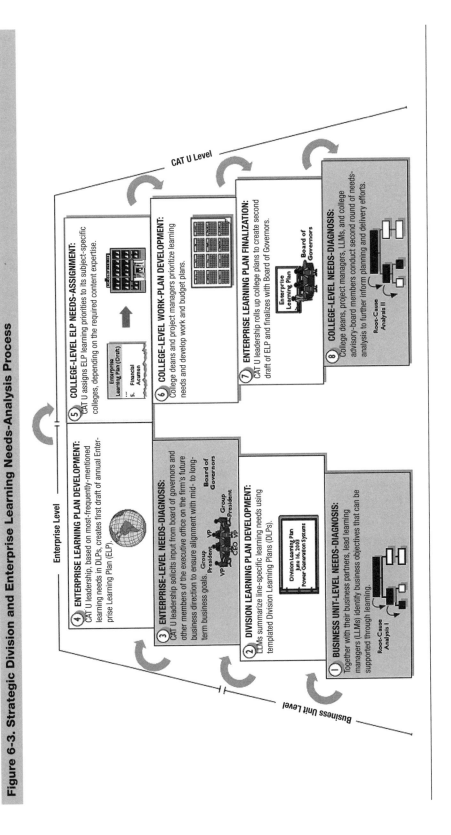

Enterprise Level

CAT U Level

Business Unit Level

4 ENTERPRISE LEARNING PLAN DEVELOPMENT: CAT U leadership, based on most-frequently-mentioned learning needs in DLPs, creates first draft of annual Enterprise Learning Plan (ELP).

5 COLLEGE-LEVEL ELP NEEDS-ASSIGNMENT: CAT U assigns ELP learning priorities to its subject-specific colleges, depending on the required content expertise.

6 COLLEGE-LEVEL WORK-PLAN DEVELOPMENT: College deans and project managers prioritize learning needs and develop work and budget plans.

3 ENTERPRISE-LEVEL NEEDS-DIAGNOSIS: CAT U leadership solicits input from board of governors and other members of the executive office on the firm's future business direction to ensure alignment with mid- to long-term business goals.

7 ENTERPRISE LEARNING PLAN FINALIZATION: CAT U leadership rolls up college plans to create second draft of ELP and finalizes with Board of Governors.

8 COLLEGE-LEVEL NEEDS-DIAGNOSIS: College deans, project managers, LLMs, and college advisory-board members conduct second round of needs-analysis to further inform planning and delivery efforts.

2 DIVISION LEARNING PLAN DEVELOPMENT: LLMs summarize line-specific learning needs using templated Division Learning Plans (DLPs).

1 BUSINESS UNIT-LEVEL NEEDS-DIAGNOSIS: Together with their business partners, lead learning managers (LLMs) identify business objectives that can be supported through learning.

Figure 6-4. Caterpillar University's Segmented Needs-Analysis Questionnaires

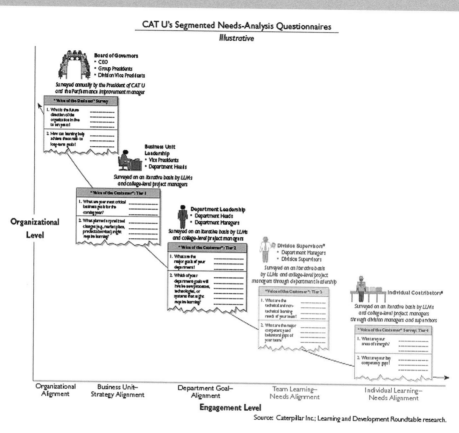

Source: Caterpillar Inc.; Learning and Development Roundtable research.

Blending Learning Technologies to Deliver Learning Interventions

Caterpillar University's introduction of technologies and the adoption of common processes and programs have produced savings. In the technology arena, for instance, Caterpillar University is the global business process owner for all learning-related systems and processes. By driving Caterpillar and its supply chain to one universal virtual collaboration tool, synchronous online learning platform, learning management system (LMS), and knowledge network, investments in these systems and processes are made once, thus avoiding duplication of effort and resources.

Caterpillar's learning management system, a Saba-based product, is an excellent example of a worldwide LMS platform (see figures 6-5a, 6-5b, and 6-5c). The newest release of Saba was implemented at the end of 2006 and serves the

Figure 6-5a. Caterpillar University's Learning Management System: ELP

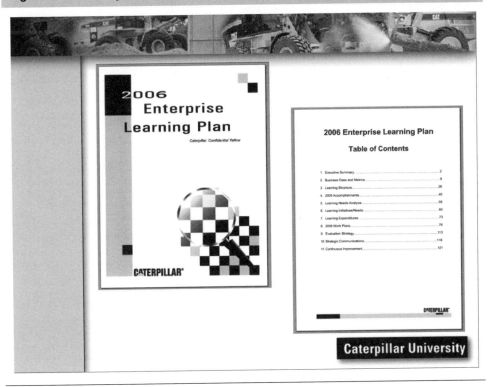

employee population, as well as the dealer network. A highly learner-centric user interface allows every individual learner to experience the LMS in a customized fashion. The user interface actually "paints" the learners' desktops with their individual learning plan (ILP). Each ILP consists of the following:

- An enterprise required learning section (built from the Enterprise Learning Plan) (see figure 6-5a)
- A business unit required learning section (built from the Division Learning Plan)
- A job role–specific learning section (built on job roles as defined by each strategy aligned business process owner) (see figure 6-5b)
- A discretionary learning section (built during the personal development discussions that occur between the employees and their leaders) (see figure 6-5c).

The culmination of these four sections allows employees to tailor their learning plan and career development plan around their current job role, as well as

Figure 6-5b. Caterpillar University's Learning Management System: Job Role Specific

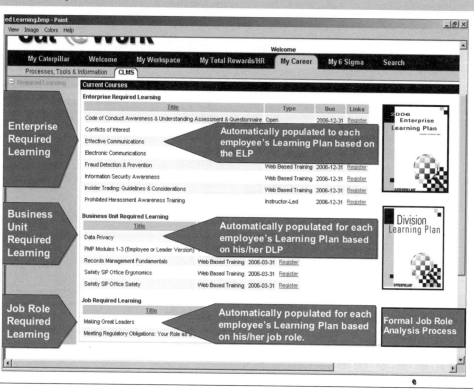

a role to which they may be aspiring. Targeting an individual's learning plan on a rifle-shot basis not only makes the most of the learner's time but reduces the learning administration significantly, thus maximizing the resources of the learner and the learning community.

From a learning delivery perspective, it is clear that our employees want to learn as part of their daily jobs. To make this a reality, job aids are delivered to employees' desktops that give them the knowledge they need when they need it and where they need it. Currently a suite of systems makes up this integrated learning environment. These systems include collaboration tools, synchronous online learning, the learning management system, and the knowledge network. Use of all of these systems has increased dramatically over the last few years:

- The number of e-lessons increased over 700 percent from 2004 through July 2006.
- The number of assessments taken online increased over 200 percent during the same time period.

Figure 6-5c. Caterpillar University's Learning Management System: Discretionary Learning

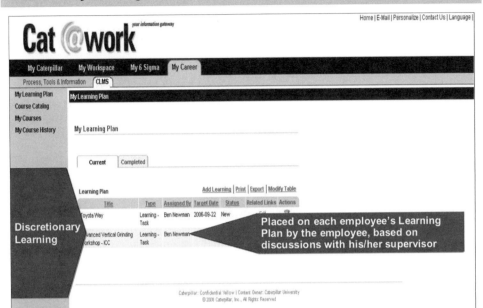

Japanese, Brazilian Portuguese, English, French, German, Italian, Russian, Simplified Chinese, Spanish

- Since its introduction into the company in 2003, the use of virtual collaboration has soared with 2006 year-end usage estimates hovering around the half million mark.
- The virtual classroom platform, introduced in late 2005, is already seeing usage at over 225 percent of expected rates.

All of these global systems allow Caterpillar to reap the benefit of cost-effective training delivery.

Evaluating the Approach

Comprehensive evaluation is a hallmark of the ELP. Once the learning initiatives to be included in the ELP are identified and agreed to by business and learning leaders, an evaluation approach is developed for each. This approach includes the college responsible for the initiative, the name of the learning initiative, and the means by which the initiative will be evaluated. All initiatives are evaluated at Level 1 (Reaction). Level 2 (Learning) evaluations are done as appropriate and are often integrated within the learning experience. Many of the ELP initiatives are evaluated at Level 3 (Application). Every year, two initiatives are evaluated at Levels 4 (Business Results) and 5 (ROI). As part of the ELP process, the evaluation approach is periodically updated.

The ELP evaluation guidelines include the following:

- All common, global learning initiatives will be evaluated in terms of how well people applied what they learned in the workplace. Application percentages were captured on Caterpillar University's Vital Factors report (scorecard) and reviewed monthly (see figure 6-6).
- The business case for a strategic initiative will include an estimate of ROI.
- Business impact and post-program ROI will be evaluated for a few initiatives selected by Caterpillar University president and CLO.

Metrics are reviewed at quarterly board of governors meetings, with decisions and required corrective actions taken accordingly.

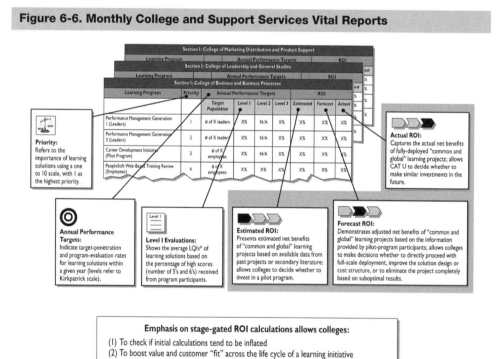

Figure 6-6. Monthly College and Support Services Vital Reports

Source: Caterpillar Inc.; Learning and Development Roundtable research.

The ELP supports budget development for learning. Each Caterpillar University college dean bases his or her annual budget and work plan on the set of ELP initiatives. Each initiative is described in terms of objectives, content/curriculum, target audience, development and deployment plan, and link to critical success factors and key business activities. Key metrics are identified, and in some cases the return-on-investment is forecast. Required funding for the initiatives is determined, and all budget summaries are rolled up into the annual business plan for Caterpillar University.

Every year, at the end of an ELP cycle, a formal process review is conducted. These "after-action reviews" are conducted with the CEO and Caterpillar University's board of governors to assess what went well and what areas require improvement. Instituting these reviews makes continuous improvement an important element of the ELP as a business process.

Impact on the Business

Using the ELP has produced important results for the organization, including the following:

- Increased collaboration between business and learning leaders to plan learning
- Improved vendor management
- Increased the strategic focus of learning
- Increased the business impact of learning
- Improved the efficiency of learning planning and reduced program redundancy
- Introduced consistency in how learning is planned for the entire enterprise
- Demonstrated the value of learning to the business.

On a larger scale, learning is now being viewed as a business activity and, as such, is being incorporated into other business processes. For example, learning is incorporated into the strategy review process at both the enterprise level and the business unit level. This ensures that learning is considered during conversations of business strategic planning and results.

The ELP has also enhanced the nature and quality of the corporate policy forming process—for example, the Strategic Planning Committee. Learning is viewed as one of the key drivers to successfully implementing the new Vision 2020.

The ELP has enabled business and learning leaders to make decisions about investing in learning initiatives that link most strongly to achieving business goals. These strong links to business goals position the learning initiatives to have a significant impact on the organization. This impact is defined in terms of intangible impact and monetary impact. The evaluation component of the ELP guides the formal evaluation of impact on the business.

Nine ROI studies showed that these learning programs, involving over 60,000 learners, will generate over $160 million in *net* benefits over a six-year period (see table 6-1).

Two-thirds of all participants in learning initiatives studied have achieved significant improvements in at least one of the following:

- Personal productivity
- Team effectiveness
- Quality of products and services
- Cost reductions
- Net revenues
- Cycle times for work processes.

Lessons Learned

The strategic alignment process has evolved and grown as a standard business practice. When this process was launched, learning leaders of each business unit (25 at the time) focused more on taking inventory of learning programs and making priority decisions based on a reduced budget allocation for learning. Input from business unit leaders was minimal. Today, however, business unit leaders are deeply engaged in making strategic decisions about learning. Recently, in an ongoing effort to continuously improve the process, the department heads (one level down from business unit leaders) have also been engaged in strategic learning planning. As a result, the alignment of learning with the business goals has never been stronger. Learning is being perceived as an integral part of achieving these business goals, and evaluation is reinforcing this message.

The evaluation strategy is a key component of aligning learning to the business goals. This strategy outlines how each of the learning initiatives will be evaluated according to the Kirkpatrick/Phillips five levels. The evaluation strategy is periodically reviewed and updated, and ROI studies have been done on selected initiatives. The business impact is evaluated in terms of the learning initiative goals, which are in turn specifically linked to the business strategy and critical success factors. Recommendations are also made to increase the business impact of the initiative. The results from all completed ROI studies are organized into a summary document that captures the ongoing value-add of learning to the business. To date,

Table 6-1. Return on Learning Summary by Year for Nine Programs Chosen for Detailed Analysis

Net Enterprise Benefits Per Year For Program and For Accumulated Over Years

Program		2002	2003	2004	2005	2006	2007	TOTAL
Assembly Training	First Year	$ 30,000	$ 135,000	$ 255,000	$ 285,000	$ 315,000	$ 345,000	$ 1,365,000
	First Two Years		$ 165,000	$ 390,000	$ 540,000	$ 600,000	$ 660,000	$ 2,385,000
	Learners	100	450	850	950	1,050	1,150	4,550
Knowledge Network	First Year	$ 2,136,900	$ 2,472,100	$ 2,807,300	$ 3,142,500	$ 3,477,700	$ 3,812,900	$ 17,849,400
	First Two Years	$ 2,136,900	$ 2,472,100	$ 2,807,300	$ 3,142,500	$ 3,477,700	$ 3,812,900	$ 17,849,400
	Parent Threads	5,100	5,900	6,700	7,500	8,300	9,100	42,600
	Dealer 1st Yr	$ 175,440	$ 657,900	$ 1,491,240	$ 1,578,960	$ 1,666,680	$ 1,754,400	$ 7,324,620
	Dealer 1st 2 Yrs	$ 175,440	$ 657,900	$ 1,491,240	$ 1,578,960	$ 1,666,680	$ 1,754,400	$ 7,324,620
	Parent Threads	80	300	680	720	760	800	3,340
Sales Training CBT	First Year	$ 114,700						$ 114,700
	First Two Years		$ 114,700					$ 114,700
	Dealer 1st Yr	$ 962,000						$ 962,000
	Dealer 1st 2 Yrs		$ 962,000					$ 962,000
	Learners	37						37
CAD Engineer WBT	First Year		$ (54,696)	$ (7,632)	$ (2,067,000)			$ (2,129,328)
	First Two Years			$ (62,328)	$ (2,074,632)			$ (2,191,656)
	Learners		86	12	3,250			3,348
Professional IT	First Year		$ 382,680	$ 540,000	$ 594,000	$ 594,000	$ 594,000	$ 2,110,680
	First Two Years			$ 922,680	$ 1,134,000	$ 1,188,000		$ 4,221,360
	Learners		1,063	1,500	1,650	1,650		5,863
On-Line English	First Year		$ (34,000)	$ (34,000)	$ (34,000)	$ (34,000)	$ (34,000)	$ (170,000)
	First Two Years		$ (34,000)	$ (34,000)	$ (34,000)	$ (34,000)	$ (34,000)	$ (170,000)
	Learners		125	125	225	225	225	925
Performance Mgmt	First Year		$ 21,741,500	$ 26,284,500	$ 10,708,500	$ 3,894,000	$ 3,894,000	$ 66,522,500
	First Two Years			$ 48,026,000	$ 36,993,000	$ 14,602,500	$ 7,788,000	$ 129,151,000
	Learners		6,700	8,100	3,300	1,200	1,200	20,500
Succeeding in Supv	First Year				$ 945,000	$ 2,160,000	$ 2,700,000	$ 5,805,000
	First Two Years					$ 3,105,000	$ 4,860,000	$ 8,910,000
	Learners				175	400	500	1,075
Hand Safety Training	First Year					$ 813,400	$ 531,200	$ 1,344,600
	First Two Years						$ 1,344,600	$ 1,344,600
	Learners					9,800	6,400	16,200

Company Total For First Year of Programs = $ 92,812,552
Company Total First Two Years = $ 161,614,404
Company Total Learners = 63,111
Dealer Total For First Year of Programs = 8,286,620
Dealer Total First Two Years = 8,286,620
Dealer Total Learners = 872
Grand Total For First Year of Programs = $ 101,099,172
Grand Total First Two Years = 169,901,024
Grand Total Learners = 63,983

Notes
1. Monetary benefits are based on actual ROI studies and projected for each year of program deployment.
2. Negative ROI results are projected for subsequent years, even though corrective actions were taken to increase the monetary return. This was done to be extra conservative in aggregating total net monetary return.

over $160 million of annualized benefits have been documented. These benefits represent bottom-line confirmation that learning is aligned to the business strategy. Whereas the learning budget was once the first to be cut during challenging business scenarios, today it is no longer disproportionately reduced, but managed as any other key business investment.

In 2007, Caterpillar University was restructured to include talent management, succession management, and organizational effectiveness functions. Going forward, the ELP will include the expanded roles and services to address the enterprise human capabilities needed to deliver Caterpillar's Vision 2020.

■ ■ ■

Leveraging the Learning Advantage

- Caterpillar's Enterprise Learning Plan features a partnership between learning and business unit leaders; a focus on driving the strategic outlook of learning; a vast scope, breadth, and global reach; and a powerful metrics and evaluation component.
- The ELP addresses issues of consistent training across business units, the involvement of company leadership in the learning planning process, a focus on business and customer need, integration with other people-related planning processes, and a rigorous evaluation process to assess the impact of learning on the business.
- Individual learning plans at Caterpillar help learners make the most of their time by giving them the knowledge they need when and where they need it. ILPs also reduce learning administration.
- The ELP has resulted in learning being viewed as a business activity at Caterpillar and being incorporated into other business practices.
- Caterpillar learning initiatives has resulted in more than $160 million in benefits over a six-year period.

7

The Case for Learning and Strategic Alignment

Karen Mantyla

Executive Summary

Key decision makers in the C suite want solid reasons for investing in training and learning initiatives. As a training professional preparing to make your case, you must make sure that you link learning objectives to the enterprise plan, identify the competencies needed to reach strategic goals, and find ways to evaluate learning programs. Presenting to key decision makers requires knowing how they like to receive information and then giving it to them in a way that helps them to understand how they will benefit from the learning plan. By understanding what is important to key decision makers, it is possible to keep a training budget intact.

Having a Plan Is Critical

When making the case for a strategic workforce development plan, it's vital to have a plan that is well thought out, as well as the polished skills necessary to present it effectively to those in the C suite. The power of persuasive presentation skills and the ability to clearly articulate the value of your workforce development plan can't be overstated.

The good news is that if your skills need polishing, you can do it. And if you already have excellent communication and persuasion skills, you have a better chance of getting buy-in and commitment from those who make the key decisions for the organization.

Those at the decision-making level want to feel confident that you've prepared sufficient data and research to back up your plan. Making a sound business decision requires that the decision makers have all of the facts. Be sure that the evaluation data show how learning aligns to organizational priorities and goals, that behavior and productivity improvements tie to the bottom line, and that organizational learning delivers results. A combination of proper preparation and excellent presentation skills will create the right climate for a "yes" for your training dollars request and help keep the dollars allocated for learning, even during budget cuts.

As stated in the Caterpillar case study, "Learning is viewed as one of the key drivers to successfully implementing the new Vision 2020." That case study illustrated what was done, who was involved, how the appeal was structured, and how tying learning to business return-on-investment (ROI) created the right mindset. It also showed what steps were taken to achieve strategic success and to keep the training budget intact.

Ten Proven Steps to Successfully Make the Case for Learning

The steps detailed in Caterpillar case study and the general steps listed here may be viewed as a good practice. But each step requires a team approach to ensure that the workforce development plan is coordinated from start to finish. It's a lot of hard work and effort, but any investment of this nature requires a solid plan of action tied to strategic desired outcomes.

Step 1: Decide on the Strategic Learning Team Structure

As you form your team, be sure to include key decision makers, such as individuals from HR, finance, and strategic planning to help the workforce development operation focus on a global view for the enterprise. Letting each person from each area know why you want him or her on the team can play a huge part in the support, commitment, and success of your plan. Including a decision maker from finance as an active member of your team from the start is especially important. This person will help you create focus areas of financial importance to the organization and ensure that they are aligned each step of the way. A finance representative can also help you create the cost-benefit analysis needed to present to the senior decision makers.

You may consider having several levels of team participation. In addition to the team described above, another group could be the key decision makers from your business units or from different operations. As the Caterpillar case study showed, the active involvement of business unit leaders was critical. Securing engagement and involvement at every level will help ensure that you are meeting the needs of the entire organization. Active engagement from the top down helps ensure that the cascade of support is in place before the plan is presented and the request for an investment and budget to remain intact is made.

The Caterpillar case study illustrated the organization of learning and governance. Each organization will have its own structure to ensure that the strategic plan covers all of the key factors. Your planning team members will also ensure that decisions are made from different perspectives throughout the enterprise. Having a governance structure helps support the plan, enables adjustments to be made as necessary, and ensures that the strategies are in continuous alignment with the strategic goals of the organization.

Step 2: Link Learning Objectives to Enterprise Plan

Ensure that the effectiveness of each learning objective and event has a strategic link to the enterprise plan, and make sure there are no kinks in the link. With each recommendation for investment, identify the strategic plan goal or objective tied to that learning link. Executives need to see the link defined. Don't expect them to make the connection on their own.

Step 3: Conduct an Effective Needs Assessment

Identify ways to conduct an effective needs assessment at every level and in every operating unit in the organization. Partner with the entire business enterprise to ensure alignment, commitment, support, and results. Starting with the top executives, ensure that all key decision makers at the executive, division, regional, and district levels are included in your needs assessment. If you have outsourced partners to support your strategic success (as was the case with the Microsoft Xbox case study in chapter 4), be sure to include an up-to-date needs assessment for the outsourced employees.

Step 4: Include Centralized Learning Units in Your Planning

Some organizations have centralized learning units. Whether they do or not, there are often strategic learning needs running through all of the operations. Determine how a centralized learning unit can support more cost-effective and meaningful training implementation at each level. Every operation thinks it is different, and every one is. Yet common thread needs span every part of each operation, especially with mandated and soft-skills training. Figures 6-5 in the Caterpillar case study offers a visual example of these common threads. At the same time, the specialized needs of every division and employee are also addressed. This is important to communicate to the division or business unit director. Many times, when an enterprise solution is presented, the reply is, "My business is different and has different needs." That's true. Yet the Caterpillar case study shows how you can overcome that objection to the centralization of a key learning plan.

Step 5: Identify Competencies for Each Strategic Goal

Be sure that you identify the competencies needed to achieve each strategic goal of the enterprise (including mandated, functional, and soft-skill competencies). Because your learning goals are linked to strategic goals, necessary competencies are those that ensure you make a solid business case for learning dollar investments.

Step 6: Use Needs Assessments to Map Out Competencies

Use the results of the needs assessment to map out the competencies needed for the internal and/or external employees and outsourced partners in each area listed above.

Step 7: Identify Current Learning Elements That Can Support Needs Assessment

It is important that you identify current learning elements or programs that may be suited to support the learning needs assessment. Be sure to include diversification of learning styles in design.

Step 8: Determine If New Learning Programs Are Needed

Determine if new learning design elements or programs need to be completed. And, as in step 7, be sure to include diversification of learning styles into design.

Step 9: Identify Appropriate Learning Technologies

Identify learning technologies that may be used for achieving learning objectives and tasks.

Step 10: Evaluate and Measure Results

Identify quantifiable metrics for evaluation of each learning program, including measurement at the five levels of the Kirkpatrick and Phillips models. Show those who make the decisions that they are getting not only a return on their investment but also a strong link to achieving the goals of the enterprise strategic plan.

Developing an Effective Workforce Development Plan

As a general guideline, as you prepare your workforce development plan you need to include these key elements:

- an executive summary
- purpose and requirements of your plan
- assessment of needs to support the strategic plan
- learning elements, course development, and support systems (including any and all technology distribution methods)
- marketing and communications
- equipment used and/or needed
- implementation process and evaluation methods
- governance structure
- cost-benefit analysis.

If you would like guidance to create a thorough workforce development plan for your organization, ASTD Press has excellent resources to support your requirement, including the *WLP Scorecard* (Rivera 2007) and *10 Steps to Successful Strategic Planning* (Barksdale & Lund 2006).

In the key elements listed above, make sure to communicate

- the mission and vision, any guiding principles and practices, goals, competitive sales, markets, and service targets
- confirmation of documented needs by key decision makers in each division or operation within the enterprise
- mapping of key competencies needed for each job in the enterprise aligned with strategic goals
- methods of training content delivery and frequency
- cost-benefit analysis for mapping to strategic goals
- roles of all team members and a workforce communications plan that keeps everyone up-to-date on needs and priorities
- timelines for marketing, training content delivery, evaluation points, and feedback input
- scorecard for keeping track of the key elements of your workforce development plan.

A further note regarding scorecards may be helpful here. You want to know how the processes are working—the key impact factors for the bottom line, including costs, measurement of learning effectiveness, feedback, and input from key stakeholders on a continuous basis. There will be specific scorecard needs for each organization. Have the scorecard readily available on your desktop for instant access and updating. Constantly monitoring the pulse of your plan reduces the number of surprises and problems that are too far along to be fixed.

Include any improvement opportunities based on current practices and any new, innovative practices that will support the success of the operation. These can be included in your plan and reflected in your cost-benefit analysis.

Each organization will have specific elements that it believes are important. These elements can be identified and included in your plan outline. The main point is to keep the alignment with the enterprise at every key angle in your plan.

As you prepare your strategic workforce development plan, ensure that you cover the basics in your planning document. Follow a logical pathway that covers all the key areas for executive knowledge and consideration (and, meets *their* learning styles—more on this later). To that end, prepare a checklist of all key result areas needed for your own organization as you prepare to present your plan.

As you work through the stages of preparation, presentation, and follow-up, you will develop checklists for areas of inclusion and documentation. Encourage members of your strategic learning team to offer their input for each of the three areas.

Preparation and Presentation

There are countless articles and books on how to prepare a plan and then make a successful presentation to senior leaders. There are also live events that showcase "how to do it." The following is not meant to be an all-inclusive primer on presentations. It is meant to highlight some critical areas of awareness when preparing and presenting your workforce development strategy plan.

Simply put, why should the C suite give you their approval and money? As with any investment, they want to be sure they understand how your plan will be in their best interests, as well as that of the organization. Having them say "yes" to what you want them to do will be the result of a carefully orchestrated process. Even though every person is different, there are certain common threads that should apply to each as they relate to presenting information and requesting money.

Remember, people buy an idea or recommendation based on *their* needs, not yours. For the C level, it's important that you understand what *they* want and need; that you show them how your plan will help *them* succeed; that you develop a trust-oriented relationship with solid facts, figures, and quantifiable metrics; and that you provide ongoing communications with them to keep your finger on the pulse of changing priorities. Discovering the emotional as well as business needs of each decision maker and presenting to those needs is important as you proceed. Whatever you do, always think about what you are doing through the eyes of the decision makers. You want to leave them with the mindset that you are a professional business advisor, not just the director of training or whatever title you may have. You are going to help them make profitable decisions, and they'll want that to happen again—and again. The end result is to achieve the strategic goals of your organization. How you meet and exceed these goals is often the result of helping those at the C level achieve their goals.

You first need to determine whether or not your organization views learning as a strategic component of its success. What is the organization's current mindset about learning? As discussed earlier in chapter 1, this is a critical aspect of a strong foundation for learning. If for any reason the organization doesn't see learning as a key driver for strategic success, figure out how you can help change the mindset from seeing learning as a pure cost factor to seeing it as a strategic investment.

There is one bottom-line result you want from the presentation of your workforce development plan and request for funding. You want a "yes" to what you are presenting, plus leadership support and commitment to make it happen in an ongoing fashion. Preparation includes carefully designing the presenting format and documents. It's not one-size-fits-all for each person listening to your presentation. Everyone is different and will absorb your information, your style of presenting, and your knowledge based on their perceptions, not on how well you present or how polished you are. Ask the executive assistants for copies of presentations used by the decision makers. You'll see how they like to have presentations prepared.

Persuasion skills are critical to business success, as evidenced by the fact that many leading universities are offering courses on persuasion skills in their undergraduate and graduate programs. Some people call these influencing skills—some call them selling skills. Whatever you call them, you need them, and you need to do them right. Remember, you only get *one chance* to make a great first impression.

There are key steps to presenting to and receiving approval from those who control the dollars spent on and invested in the enterprise. Whether you have incredible experience and expertise in effectively presenting to senior decision makers, or you have little or no experience, the following tips can be useful in getting people to say "yes." They cover the basics. Yet sometimes the basics are forgotten.

As you prepare for and build your presentation, be sure to know the following:

- Your subject matter and design of presenting your knowledge. Ask yourself how you will communicate
  - key aspects of the enterprise strategic plan
  - results of a thorough needs assessment for the workforce development plan
  - selection of learning content and delivery methods
  - alignment with the enterprise strategic goals and objectives
  - evaluation methods
  - metrics for success.
- The people who make the decisions:
  - Who are they?
  - What weight do they carry in decision making?
  - What areas are most important to *them*?
  - What learning styles are represented in the C suite?
  - How do they like their data presented?
  - How will your plan support *their* success?

The importance of excellent preparation and presentation design can't be overstated. You may want to use a blended learning approach for designing and delivering your content. Your decision makers should always be the driving force for your preparation. You can't get your training budget approved, and keep it, without their approval.

To continue, you will also want to know how to develop your presentation effectively. Make sure to identify key delivery information:

- How has the presentation been positioned to those at the C level?
- What are their expectations?
- What is the format they prefer when receiving presentations?
- How many people will be there, and what are their learning styles? This may be a tough question, yet a critical one in deciding how to present your data. Figure out what kind of charts and visuals they like and then design your presentation to address all learning styles. You can use your own checklists for presenting to different learning styles, or use Craig Mindrum's tips from chapter 8.

What about work behavioral styles? Taking behavior styles into account can be an incredible opportunity to create a presentation that resonates with the decision makers. Knowing these different styles allows you to modify your own behavior to support successful outcomes of those who have a significant impact on your success. People making decisions are not thinking about changing their behavior to suit your preferred work behavioral style. It's up to you to assess *their* style, then be sure that you know how to present to them. People usually write or present based on their own preferred style. If you feel that way, change your mindset. It's not about you, it's about them. Communication casualties usually occur when people don't know how to modify their own behavior to support the needs of others.

Often we are not privy to any formal assessment tools used for the senior executives. Yet if we listen and watch, some similar behavioral characteristics emerge. Knowing the behavioral style, learning style, and preferred method of receiving data is the key to knowing your decision makers. While we don't often conduct a personal styles needs assessment to see how we should present to others, it's important to be aware of how this affects your success. We don't want to generalize or stereotype, but common behaviors are often seen among the C-level cadre. For tips on how to present to styles frequently seen in the C suite, see the sidebars.

Presenting to Dominant Decision Makers

Dominant behavior styles are common in senior decision makers. Many military leaders have this style because of the work that they are required to do, but dominant styles are also prevalent in other sectors including private, government, education, and not-for-profit. With these dominant, fast-moving strategic thinkers, often termed "Alpha males or females," it's critical to know how to tailor your presentation in a way that speaks to them.

Many of those with a dominant style value directness, winning, and results. They don't like people telling them what to do. Give them options—pros and cons—and let them know that you'll be guided by their decision. Never argue with a dominant personality—you'll lose. Don't react emotionally if they do not immediately accept what you are saying. People who possess dominant behavior also get impatient with those who seem hesitant, less than confident, and who make them look at every chart and detail in the book. They like you to tell them the bottom-line results up front, how you'll get there, what you need from them, and when you need it: in other words, bullet, bullet, bullet. You can have the in-depth details with you for reference, but focus on the bottom line.

Alpha males or females tend to view change as business as usual, and they think and work at the speed of light. Ready, aim, fire. "Start with the end in mind" for them, as well as everyone else, as Stephen Covey stated many years ago. It would be prudent to begin with a statement such as, "By the end of our presentation, we will justify investing $___ for a workforce development plan linked to strategic success." Then, lead your audience down a short, logical pathway that shows how you will achieve this. Attaching a complete package of information to your presentation, versus going through every detail, will help answer questions for those who are more detail oriented. Be sure you have a table of contents for easy access to specific information. Going through too many details, unless asked, will make your dominant-style decision makers restless.

Presenting to Detail-Oriented Decision Makers

Detail-oriented decision makers will look for thorough research, data, and specific information based on your presentation and recommendations. For them, everything needs to be documented in a logical, step-by-step fashion. They usually work at a slower pace than dominant-style decision makers because they like to take time to analyze data. They do not like to rush to a decision. Being thorough and looking at every minute detail are often important to them. Sometimes, these detail-oriented thinkers take *too* long to make a decision. Negotiated deadlines can help move the process along. These people focus on quality, accuracy, and order. They take time to calculate the risks thoroughly, sometimes to the point of paralyzing themselves by analysis. They often look at something many times to ensure that it is "perfect." They will analyze both your data and your methods of presenting the data to ensure that you have been thorough and accurate.

When presenting to a detail-oriented decision maker, make sure you have all the facts and have checked for accuracy. It's often helpful to prepare an advance package of data that backs up your recommendations and can be given to those who will make the final decisions.

Proactive Follow-Up

Successful organizations provide excellent service to their customers. This is important to achieving customer satisfaction. Your decision makers are your customers, and they will determine if they are satisfied or not.

Monitoring the pulse of the needs and requirements of your decision makers is a must in this fast-changing world. You will be best served if you have a proactive follow-up service plan document that answers how you will do the following:

- Stay on top of the changing needs of the organization.
- Monitor the pulse of the changing needs of the decision makers.
- Identify the different needs of the workforce, both internal and external.
- Use technology to support any changing needs.
- Update the workforce development plan to support changes (this is a living document).
- Have a communication process for continuous feedback flow from all key stakeholders.

In addition, you might want to mention your follow-up service plan in your presentation of your workforce development plan. This shows that you care enough to devote the time to provide follow-up service to those you serve.

Presenting to Mixed Audiences

You will often have both dominant as well as detail-oriented decision makers in your presentations. Prepare a table of contents for your documents to help the fast-moving, dominant individuals go to exactly what they want to see and show the detail-oriented people that you've covered all the bases. Some people even give out advance copies of their presentations and documents. Because every organization is different, you will need to understand your organization's policies and preferences to make the most effective presentations.

In follow-up service, identify areas that are critical to keeping on top of all factors that affect the learning needs of the workforce. Mergers, acquisitions, changing roles, new decision makers, new markets, rules, regulations, policies, reorganizations, hiring, transformations, outsourcing, downsizing, and new technology all have an impact on your plan. Thinking ahead to create this service plan will give those in the C suite more confidence in viewing you as a valued strategic partner.

Alert your key stakeholders to new ways to address changing priorities and how changing course, if necessary, benefits them. Your ability to forecast an opportunity or even danger sign could mean the difference between profit and loss. Your key decision makers will appreciate knowing that you are on the constant lookout for ways to support them in a changing environment, *especially when they don't have to ask*.

In his book on trends in HR, Tom R. Knighton noted that "Leaders want to shorten the time from learning to action" (Knighten 2007). What this means is that you want to do everything to stay ahead of the curve to support the enterprise needs for workforce development. Being agile in thought, process, and action will keep you focused on your internal and external customer needs. In the short and long term, proactively monitoring the pulse on those needs will help both you and your plan succeed. You'll reach the bottom line for the enterprise and help to keep your training budget intact.

■ ■ ■

Leveraging the Learning Advantage

- Develop a workforce development strategic team, and involve key decision makers in the organization to participate.
- Thoroughly understand the strategic plan of the enterprise, and link learning objectives to that plan.

- Evaluate learning goals with business impact metrics to illustrate to key decision makers the ROI and the link to meeting the goals of the enterprise learning plan.
- Know and align your plan with the key decision makers in the C suite; prepare and present your plan to them effectively.
- Provide proactive follow-up service to executive decision makers as if they were your customers—because they *are*.

■■■■ **8**

Learning Styles

A Critical Component for Successful Learning Design and Delivery

Craig Mindrum,
Strategic and Talent Management Consultant

Executive Summary

A learning event can only be effective if it is based on an awareness of basic human cognition—how participants think and learn. And people learn differently, with varied preferences for interacting with learning content. Today, many learning departments are missing opportunities to increase the effectiveness of learning experiences by failing to offer courses that can be consumed in different ways, depending on how a particular individual learns—that is, according to the person's *learning style*.

Innovators in enterprise learning are increasingly designing environments that can be both centrally driven, from the top down, and learner driven, from the bottom up. Learning *content* must be informed by what people need to know and do to execute organizational goals. But the learning *experience* must be designed with the flexibility to accomodate differences in how people learn.

The variety of choices available through e-learning increases the chances of matching learning experiences with an individual's own style of thinking and learning. By aligning learning design with the unique thinking and learning styles of people, or of a particular workforce, companies can increase their return on learning investment and realize measurable business improvements.

What's Your Style?

Recently a colleague and I were both speakers at the same learning conference. While I dutifully sat and pretended to pay attention to the other presentations (more about that in a moment), my associate seemed to disappear for long stretches of time. As I looked out the window at the beautiful countryside in the south of France on a gorgeous sunny day, I was uncertain whether to be irritated by or envious of whatever he was doing.

As it turns out, he was indeed outside, taking walks through the hills. But not just idly meandering. He had found a way to take materials he wanted to read—academic papers, articles, and book chapters—scan them, run them through a text-to-speech program, and load them on his iPod. So he was working, I suppose. Or listening. Or something.

Although I was impressed that this fellow, with graduate degrees in a number of obscure and arcane academic areas, could perform such a technological feat, I listened with only half an ear to the details of how he had done it. I knew it wasn't for me. I have been unable to take advantage of even the most modest of audio learning technologies. Some years back, when my commute to work could sometimes be an hour each way, I tried listening to books on tape—only to find that I was forever having to rewind them because my mind had wandered for unknown stretches of time.

I'm the guy who, walking out of church, cannot tell you much of anything that the minister preached about 10 minutes ago. Or the one who, to return to the subject of conference presentations, harbors a secret and currently unfashionable love of PowerPoint—because it forces otherwise rambling oratory into a few moments of clarity based on something I can read. Give me bullet points or give me death. And don't even get me started on the value of teleconference calls (for my learning style, that is).

The point here is not to belabor my own idiosyncrasies; it is simply to state a truth that all learning professionals know, but which is—for now, at least—dramatically underleveraged by most organizations and their learning departments: people learn in different ways. Although we share a great deal in common simply by having the same genetic code, our brains process information differently. We have different thinking styles or cognitive styles; therefore, we have different learning styles, as well. You're detail oriented; I like the big picture. You like images; I like words. You prefer to work in solitude; I like to hash things out in conversation.

For example, some people are better with auditory learning. Others (myself included) are better visual and verbal learners. Still others are kinesthetic learners—they learn best in a hands-on, learn-by-doing mode. Then there are multimodal learners, who possess some combination of styles.

The *theoretical* relevance of learning styles to professionals in this area needs no justification; if you're a learning professional, you need to be cognizant of *how* people learn, period. The question, instead, is this: Does the awareness of different thinking and learning styles have value that can really shape how enterprise learning events are delivered on a day-to-day basis, given the other demands on their time and the other mandates they struggle to meet?

Learning executives today face growing pressures to demonstrate business relevance and impact. One research study for which I helped perform an analysis a couple of years ago showed that the number-one challenge learning executives face today—beyond even dealing with limited budgets—is measuring the effectiveness of learning from a business standpoint. If you're trying to approximate a kind of rapid, factory approach to learning delivery, the intricacies of individual learning styles are likely to be overlooked or at least tabled for a later day. Indeed, the title of one seminal book on learning styles—Mel Levine's *A Mind at a Time*—sounds almost like a threat in the corporate environment (Levine 2003).

Given today's emphasis on the business impact of learning, I wasn't surprised that my own research found that approximately zero percent of corporate learning executives are using the concept of learning styles to any degree in their planning and their day-to-day work. I am exaggerating, of course—at least, I think I am. My "survey" was an informal, unscientific set of emails I sent to about two dozen friends and colleagues in the learning field. Yet there is significance in the fact that not a single person wrote back to tell me that the concept of learning styles was influencing the current work of his or her department in any real way. Here is a sample of the responses:

- "I am not looking at learning styles right now. I'm more focused on getting the enterprise level function up and running."
- "I'm so busy just trying to put some basic structures in place across the company that this isn't even on my radar screen at the moment…and I don't expect it to be for some time."
- "It has become challenging enough just to stay afloat of all the systems and process enhancements."

Understandable. And yet, think for a moment of the hidden business cost of the reality that learning departments are designing courses without much attention to the manner in which their employees as individuals optimally learn. The conclusion one reaches after just a few minutes with the copious literature on learning styles is that much of what learning departments develop today for their employees washes over many of them like rain on a waterproof jacket. In other words, a great deal of corporate learning is either a waste of money or is delivering only a small portion of the potential return-on-investment. And if one believes that enterprise learning is one way to engage employees and help retain them, then the human resource costs associated with poor learning experiences need to be added to the debit side of the equation as well.

Which leads me to the thesis that I will defend here: The concepts of thinking styles and learning styles actually provide both the business context for maximizing the effect of learning on workforce performance and the learning context that helps one effectively apply new learning technologies, such as virtual collaboration, podcasting, and blogging, directing them toward optimal business ends.

An effective learning experience must be designed simultaneously from the top down and the bottom up. From the top down, strategy informs the content that must be learned and the workforce behaviors that are needed. However, more advanced, learner-driven environments require the mode of content delivery and the technology choices to be informed by learning styles if learning events are to maximize the effect on people and the impact on overall business performance.

From the bottom up, an understanding of people and their performance needs supports a learner-driven strategy that can drive innovation and optimize the return on learning investment.

Avoiding the Coming Crisis?

The appropriate application of thinking styles and learning styles theory can also reinvigorate a learning profession that is reeling a bit from the demands to look at all learning development from a predominantly business perspective. No one is saying that applying business outcome analysis to learning is a bad thing. The question is whether the pendulum has swung too far. One might argue that the balance was once tilted too much toward instructional design and learning delivery for their own sake, without enough emphasis on the effects that learning has. But is a CFO perspective alone ultimately best for enterprise learning?

I recently attended a major conference on learning trends where one of the attendees said to me, "If I have to sit through one more conference session on measurement, I'm going to scream." During the discussion period at another session, this one on innovative learning technologies, I brought up the subject of learning styles. Many faces in the room lit up, and the ensuing dialogue was energized and lively. "Thanks for bringing up a topic that energizes us" was the message I took away from the experience.

I also spoke with a manager—highly educated and experienced in learning theory and practice—who expressed dismay that so many colleagues in her department had little formal background in the field. On a personal level, she was feeling increasingly isolated—not only that her input could not be understood, but that her bosses were actually antagonistic to her point of view. On a professional level, she worried that customers were being ill-served because decisions about learning delivery were being made, not for the wrong reasons, but for incomplete reasons. Efficiency and effectiveness do not always go hand in hand.

This is anecdotal evidence, to be sure. But the atrophying of deep learning knowledge and skills among corporate learning departments, if it is occurring, should be a cause for concern. One way to counter this trend would be to provide a business perspective at a more detailed level within the field of corporate learning. Rather than look only at the business impact of "learning" broadly conceived, we should also ask what the business relevance and impact are of specific components of learning theory and practice—in this case, learning styles and thinking styles. This specificity would deepen the potential impact of enterprise learning and prevent business executives from mistakenly believing that the essential building blocks of world-class learning experiences are "just details."

An Overview of Styles

The theoretical background of the subject of learning styles takes one through a number of storied names in education, philosophy, and psychology—Carl Jung, Jean Piaget, John Dewey, William James, Carl Rogers, and many others. More recently, Howard Gardner, Anthony Gregorc, Mel Levine, and David Kolb, to name just a few, have made significant additions to the field.

A full discussion of the various perspectives on learning and cognitive styles is beyond the scope of this chapter. One set of researchers did a literature scan and claimed more than 70 different theories are in existence (Coffield et al. 2004). But the central idea is straightforward: People think in different ways and, therefore, also learn in different ways. As one researcher puts it, we are apt to underestimate these differences and overestimate the extent to which everyone else thinks the same way we do or acquires knowledge as we do (Sternberg 1997, 18).

The fact that one person's brain may process and apply information in a different way from another person's brain results in various kinds of tragedies both small and large in different domains. In relationships, such differences lead to misunderstandings, poor communication, delays in resolving differences, and even animosity. In education, a pedagogy centered on teachers and content rather than on students and the manner in which individuals learn optimally may result in classroom experiences that are aligned only with the way the teacher learns best. Teachers may misdiagnose a "problem" student or one who appears slow when, in fact, the student is merely waiting for someone to bring his or her mind alive in the right way.

In the corporate world, we also see the effects of an insufficient understanding of thinking and learning styles. From a career choice and development point of view, people may end up in jobs that they seem to desire, but which are not a good fit for them, given the way they process and apply information. In the field of enterprise learning, stylistic differences can cause some employees to learn more slowly, even if they are otherwise bright and able. The time to competency for a portion of the workforce might be unnecessarily high, with measurable cost impacts. More generally, development time and resources on learning vehicles may be wasted because those vehicles may not be appropriate for the learning audience—or may only be appropriate for a percentage of that audience.

One of the biggest insights that crops up in reading through the literature on thinking and learning styles—and discussing this topic with practitioners—is that teachers, trainers, and managers are forever confusing ability with thinking/learning styles. A style is a preferred set of ways in which someone processes information. It is not an ability, but a preferred manner of applying one's abilities.

In the corporate world—according to a sort of consensus of the psychological research—abilities account for only about 10 percent of the variation among workers in job performance (Sternberg 1997, 8-9). That is an astounding number. Even if it's wrong by a factor of five, its impact would hardly be weakened. If abilities accounted for 50 percent of variation in job performance, it would still lead to the same unsettling conclusion: Corporate learning departments may not only be teaching the wrong content (focused on knowledge, skills, and abilities, but not styles), but teaching it in the wrong ways.

How might enterprise learning departments design learning programs to affect the huge variance in job performance? The company that can crack that one will generate unbelievable leaps in employee productivity. And learning and cognitive styles would be one key part of cracking the code.

As I walk through some highlights of learning/cognitive style theory and research, here is the logical progression I will follow:

- **Neurodevelopmental background.** Human beings are made up of multiple neurodevelopmental systems that integrate to form a whole person. Because of genetic and environmental factors, these subsystems operate at different strengths in different people.
- **Thinking styles.** Based on the strength of those neurodevelopmental systems, people have preferred ways of interacting with stimuli and processing information. This fact has a number of implications for sourcing and developing employees, as well as for leadership development. An awareness of cognitive styles can help leaders provide more specific guidance, coaching, and mentoring to those with whom they work.
- **Learning styles.** Learning, being one form of cognition, is therefore also affected by the status of a person's neurodevelopmental systems and preferred thinking styles. Awareness of the thinking and learning styles dominant in one particular type of workforce could help training departments devise more focused learning experiences that result in greater impact in less time. Making certain core training available in different modes (for example, in one format for a visual learner, in another for an auditory one) has the potential to dramatically improve the impact of enterprise learning on workforce performance.

Neurodevelopmental Systems

In *A Mind at a Time*, Mel Levine likens our minds to tool chests, filled with delicate instruments—our neurodevelopmental systems—which are the implements we use to learn and to apply what we've learned (Levine 2003). He writes, "Just as a carpenter might deploy different groups of tools to complete various projects or a dentist might use different sets of tools for different tooth tasks, our minds make use of different clusters of neurodevelopmental functions to learn specific skills and to create particular products" (Levine 2003, 35).

Although, with about 30 million synapses in the average adult brain, the number of neurodevelopmental connections is almost infinite, these can be grouped into eight primary neurodevelopmental systems. That means that any student or employee is participating in a learning experience using a range of brain functions, which according to Levine (2003) include the following:

- **Attention control system.** Directs the distribution of mental energy in our brains; the headquarters for the mental regulators that control learning and behavior.
- **Memory system.** Stores and delivers information as needed.
- **Language system.** Detects meaningful differences in human sounds; controls the capacity to express thoughts while speaking, writing, or using gestures and other symbols.
- **Spatial ordering system.** Controls our ability to perceive how parts of things fit together and helps us organize physical objects we need. Also enables us to think with images.
- **Sequential ordering system.** Helps us deal with the chains of information that come into or depart from our minds coded in a particular sequence.
- **Motor system.** Governs the precise and complex network of tight connections between the brain and various muscles in the body.
- **Higher thinking system.** Regulates the capacity to solve problems and reason logically, to form and make use of concepts, to understand how and when rules apply, and to get the point of a complicated idea. Includes critical and creative thinking.
- **Social thinking system.** Controls the ability to sense and build on social cues to form relationships and to work collaboratively.

These systems interact in ways that enable us to accomplish different things at different times. If you're a mechanic, your attention control, memory, spatial, and sequential order systems combine with your motor system to help you take apart an engine, fix it, and put it back together. And consider what happens during an average business meeting. You've got your attention control, memory, language, spatial and sequential ordering, higher thinking, and social thinking systems all working at once. No wonder meetings are exhausting. And no wonder that two people coming out of the same meeting can sometimes have such dramatically different impressions. The sequential thinker needed information, got it, and now is ready to get on with the tasks ahead. The thinker focused on social dimensions noticed some troubling relationships among the meeting attendees and is worried about how everything is going.

Once we see the fact that these multiple systems are in place within our brains, we can more fully appreciate the insights coming from someone like Howard Gardner regarding multiple kinds of intelligences (Gardner 1993). People can excel within some of these systems but not in others. Some are especially gifted in verbal-linguistic areas or in music. Others excel at logical-mathematical activities. World-class athletes are particularly good at spatial and bodily-kinesthetic activities. Most politicians and certain types of business people are adept at the interpersonal and social aspects of intelligence.

This last area—what Levine calls the social thinking system—is particularly influential in how people feel about themselves as they enter the workforce and is also a large determinant of their overall career success in a corporate environment. "Those who have stunted functions for social interaction," Levine writes, "are condemned to feel the pain of exposure and daily humiliation. They are likely to be the most downtrodden students in a school (and also the most anguished employees on the job)" (Levine 2003, 35).

Thinking Styles

Just as a person with a sore left elbow will compensate by trying to carry most things with the right arm, the relative strengths of our various neurodevelopmental systems will cause us to favor some forms of mental activity over others. We will develop certain styles—which, once again, are not our abilities, but the manner in which we apply our abilities. As another definition has it, our cognitive style is our "preferred and habitual method to organizing and representing information" (Riding & Rayner 1998, 15). Listen closely to how someone restates a point during a meeting or learning experience ("Are you saying that …") and you might see this point at work. "I heard what you said, but according to how I think, this is how I'm choosing to interpret and store that information."

It will probably come as no surprise to learn that multiple models of thinking styles exist. Some approaches look at perceptual modalities—how people react to stimuli from their environment, and how they assimilate data. Others look at how people process information—how they perceive, organize, and retain it. Still others focus on certain patterns of human personalities, especially as they reflect our emotions and values. Carl Jung was one of the first who advanced this way of understanding human perception and behavior. In Jung's personality theory, people can be classified as sensing individuals, intuitives, thinkers, and feeling individuals (Jung 1923).

Within these basic model types are a wide range of options. However, since one of my personal thinking styles tends toward the global (that is, a preference for large, abstract issues) and not the local (a preference for concrete, detailed issues), I won't spend a lot of time on the details and would refer the reader to any of the books mentioned in this chapter (and the many, many others not mentioned).

But here are a few examples: Some people think in a way that is exploratory and open-ended; others are more focused and close-ended. Some are impulsive, while others are reflective. I have a friend who is an engineer, and who is apt to place new information into an existing framework of what he knows. Another friend, a mountain climber, craves the unknown and will purposely seek out knowledge and experiences beyond her comfort level.

Or, consider colleagues and bosses you have known who reach decisions quickly after a brief consideration of options (they're the impulsives), compared with others who deliberate extensively before arriving at conclusions (the reflectives). On another scale, some of our colleagues tend to be single-minded; others can multitask and still maintain order because they can prioritize from a list of multiple tasks; and still others (we know who we are) are "all over the place" most of the time.

Another thinking styles spectrum—intuitive versus analytic—is a favorite when discussions of gender differences arise. Some people know something to be true without breaking it down into parts first—they know it is true without knowing exactly why. Others seek to decompose an issue or idea before they will assent to its truth or relevance.

Robert Sternberg (1997) provides helpful guidance in avoiding the dangers of misunderstanding or oversimplifying thinking styles and then applying them inappropriately. For example:

- We don't have a single style, but a set of preferred styles. Don't be "monarchic" (as one thinking styles scale has it) when it comes to this topic and err toward seeing things unidimensionally. Don't pigeonhole people. Also, he says, don't make illusory correlations. Creative people aren't necessarily messy, for example. (Sternberg obviously has not seen my home office.) In spite of my earlier examples, not all engineers are assimilators; not all mountain climbers are explorers from a cognitive styles point of view. And my earlier remark about one gender being more intuitive, the other more analytic? Another illusory correlation. I think.
- We might have one preferred style in one environment and a different style for a different situation. A disinterest in instruction manuals gets me into trouble all the time while putting together my kids' toys. But in the kitchen, I am perfectly content following a recipe.
- Strength and pervasiveness of preferences are important factors, as well. Some people have a slight preference for a particular kind of work environment. For example, all things being equal, they'd prefer a livelier, noisy environment. Others may have very strong preferences. I suspect that the move toward telecommuting is having profound but incompletely understood effects on the

engagement of employees, as some of them struggle to accommodate their inherent thinking styles under new conditions where they are staring only at their computer screens for hours and days each week.

- Our styles may change as we get older and accumulate different experiences. If you took a Myers-Briggs test many years ago, you might want to take another one. Our experiences change us. Were I to cook enough, perhaps I would no longer be content following someone else's recipes and would become more creative. We would do well to ingrain the concept that "people change" into our leadership development courses. That person you formed an impression of several years ago when she was first starting out? She is not the same person five years later when your paths cross again.

Perhaps the most important point to make about styles in the context of this chapter is that styles are teachable. One can encourage the styles needed to succeed by developing learning programs or assigning people to tasks that require them to develop those styles. Two extremes need to be avoided when considering learning/cognitive styles in a corporate environment. One extreme says there's nothing we can do, because people are who they are. Yes, they have tendencies and preferences. But, in many cases, they can be taught different styles.

At the other extreme is a sense that we should be able to be all things to all people, and that we can find endless ways to accommodate any differences in styles. In fact, that's not true—at least not in the real world of limited time and resources. Certain jobs, for example, require a well-developed social system and a style that accommodates collaboration. We can try as much as reason and time permit to help people develop a better collaborative thinking style. Thinking styles *can* be taught, but that doesn't mean everyone wants to be taught or wants to change. An intransigent loner, for example, may need to be counseled out of a job or even out of the organization itself.

In a corporate environment, the ability to understand the thinking styles needed to succeed in a particular job or role and then to select people based on their apparent match for that style are important aspects of successful recruiting and sourcing. Diagnostics such as the Myers-Briggs test have been used for years to help organizations assess the fit of a recruit to a particular job. I am nervous, I must confess, about the overreliance on such tests as the only input to the first stage of recruiting. They overemphasize one style (analytics) and underemphasize other styles, such as the intuition about people that a good interviewer may develop. However, used properly, such assessments can help organizations select the right people for the right jobs. They can also help people understand themselves better—something that I will argue later must be a component of what learning departments provide for employees.

What has not happened in most corporate settings, however, is the more general use of thinking styles theory in corporate leadership development, where a sensitivity to such issues would enhance a manager's ability to provide effective coaching and mentoring. Sternberg tells the story of José, a successful software designer for a high-tech company. José was a terrific designer, but he wanted something more; he wanted to manage. Eventually, he got his wish. The problem was that he wasn't very good at managing. It wasn't a matter of ability. It was a matter of thinking styles. José was a bit disorganized and preferred working by himself—something that had served him well as a designer, but not as a manager who needs to show interest in subordinates and help them develop (Sternberg 1997).

The right mentor or career counselor might have been able to help José, either by getting him the right kind of training to develop the styles necessary to realize his career aspirations, or by moving him into a position better suited to his existing styles and helping him understand where his strengths really resided.

Here is an opportunity to apply the "top down and bottom up" approach that is ultimately at the heart of the position I am advocating about the role of learning styles in developing high-impact corporate learning. One could well argue that traditional leadership development is primarily a top-down endeavor: We acquire basic leadership skills, which we apply uniformly across a section of the workforce who works with us or for us. But unless we simultaneously take a bottom-up understanding of the individual needs and styles of those people, our general principles will work only with the portion of the workforce whose styles are amenable to what we are doing.

What is the difference between a manager applying unitary leadership principles and a teacher attempting to teach every student the same way? They are both top-down approaches that desperately need a corresponding bottom-up understanding and sensitivity if they are to produce optimal results.

Learning Styles

At this point, given the swirl of frameworks, models, and theories already at work in this chapter, just a few examples of learning styles research should suffice to make the point.

VAK Model. Consider, first, the family of learning styles models referred to at the beginning of this chapter, sometimes abbreviated as VAK for "visual-auditory-kinesthetic." Some people learn best by looking, others by listening, and others by doing. A fourth category—reading/writing—is sometimes added for people who learn best by processing text (and, yes, the acronym then becomes VARK). Some learners have a single mode by which they learn optimally; others are multimodal, meaning they are strong in more than one category. In general, all human beings are multimodal to an extent—at least in the sense that we need variety to hold our interest and to reinforce things we have learned in different modes. The rise of blended learning design in recent years is a testament to the ability of multimodal learning to have a superior impact on workforce performance.

Variations of this model, which is based on different input modalities, can be found among numerous educators and practitioners. One that I particularly like posits four categories of learners in different combinations:

- **Visual/verbal.** People with this dominant style learn best when information is presented visually and in a written-language format. They like to see present-ers reinforce points made orally by writing them on a blackboard or showing them on a slide deck.
- **Visual/nonverbal.** These people learn best when information is presented visually and in a picture or design format. These kinds of learners come alive when a presenter illustrates points with a video or a chart.
- **Auditory/verbal.** Those with this dominant style enjoy listening to a speech or lecture, live or on audiotape. They also enjoy speaking and listening with others in a learning environment.
- **Tactile/kinesthetic.** People with this style learn best when they can roll up their sleeves and get their hands into an activity. These learners love live demonstrations and field work. Performance simulations are especially good for kinesthetic learners, since they allow people to practice actual behaviors needed to succeed at their jobs. Although this style is, on the one hand, a par-ticular one preferred by some learners, the use of tactile/kinesthetic activities is important in any extended learning experience to reinforce and augment what might otherwise be a primarily auditory and visual mode of learning.

David Kolb and the Learning Styles Inventory. David Kolb, an important figure in the development of experiential learning, developed a theory of learning styles in the 1970s and 1980s that still enjoys a great deal of influence (see figure 8-1). Kolb based his Learning Styles Inventory on two different sets of variables:

- **How people take in information:** Do they prefer concrete experience or abstract conceptualization?
- **How people internalize information:** Do they prefer active experimenta-tion or reflective observation?

Figure 8-1. David Kolb's Experiential Learning Cycle

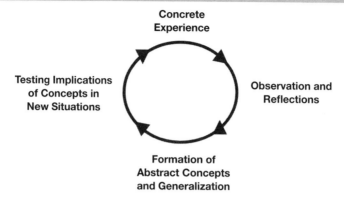

Creating a two-by-two matrix based on those sets of variables results in four learning styles (figure 8-2):

- **Concrete-reflective (divergers).** These learners need to be personally engaged in learning activities. They want to know how course material relates to their work, interests, and careers.
- **Abstract-reflective (assimilators).** The characteristic question from these learners is not "why?" but "what?" They often need to follow detailed, sequential steps in a learning activity. They like things presented logically and need time for reflection to benefit fully from a learning experience.
- **Abstract-active (convergers).** Such learners need to be involved in pragmatic problem-solving activities during a learning event. They generally seek to work interactively on well-defined tasks and to learn by trial and error in an environment that allows them to fail safely.
- **Concrete-active (accommodators).** These learners like to "fiddle with the dials." Tell them the way something should be done and they're likely to respond, "Yes, but what if …" They're risk takers. They want to apply course material in new ways, experiment with things, and make changes. More than the others, such learners need flexibility in how a learning experience is conducted.

Anthony Gregorc developed a variation on the Kolb model in the 1980s. Gregorc concurs with Kolb on the "concrete versus abstract" variable in learning, but he substitutes "sequential versus random" for the second variable (Gregorc 2006).

Figure 8-2. Four Types of Learners within Kolb's Learning Styles Model

Concrete

Accommodator	Diverger
• Trial-and-error style • Interested in action and results • Adapts well to immediate circumstances • Sets objectives • Sets schedules	• Imaginative; good at generating ideas • Can view situation from different angles • Open to experience • Investigates • Senses opportunities
Converger	**Assimilator**
• Good at practical applications • Does well when there is one answer • Evaluates plans • Selects from alternatives • Makes decisions	• Strong at creating theoretical models • Defines problems • Compares alternatives • Establishes criteria • Formulates hypotheses

Abstract

Active ←—————————————————→ Reflective

Source: Adapted from "Learning cycles and learning styles: Kolb's experiential learning theory and its application in geography in higher education," by Mick Healey and Alan Jenkins. *Journal of Geography,* 99, pp. 185-195. Used with permission.

That is, some people are more comfortable following an orderly path through material, while others prefer trial and error—they like hashing things out in energetic conversation that might skip from one subject to another. They enjoy an almost serendipitous approach to education and seeing how insights arise from the spontaneous work of a group.

This latter variable is of particular interest to me, because it represents my own blind spot as a university teacher for more than 15 years. At the beginning of every course I have taught, I have warned students that they should not expect to come out of the term with a nice notebook of lecture notes containing the "truth." I am a random, active learner myself. I like floating ideas out and having conversations, exposing the ideas to multiple viewpoints to watch them morph or even die from lack of support. That is also how I teach. I make abundant use of small groups and other activities where students are expected to engage with the material and converse with each other (and with me).

But, if I were to be honest with myself, what am I doing except forcing my own learning style on my students? In what respect am I failing the abstract-reflective or concrete-sequential students? Although I have made no dramatic shifts in my classes based on this awareness, I have nevertheless introduced more variety into my pedagogy, such as offering short lectures on certain topics. I also end most classes by summing up major points on the blackboard, thus accommodating my visual-verbal students and others who might otherwise go home wondering what, in fact, they actually "learned."

Implications: Top Down and Bottom Up

As I noted at the beginning of the chapter, learning and HR executives are under increasing pressure today to demonstrate the business impact of their work. Indeed, it's this pressure that (again, based on my unscientific survey) appears to be preventing learning professionals from applying cognitive/learning styles theories to their work in any appreciable way. "I can barely keep up with the mandates given to me to get content out to our most important employees," learning executives appear to be saying. "The application of learning styles is a luxury I can't afford right now."

Yet my position is that running learning like a business needs the idea of learning styles, and vice versa. How can a company deliver training that results in measurable business improvements—better customer satisfaction and retention, increased sales and revenue, and so forth—unless learning professionals can be sure that the training can be absorbed and applied by employees in ways to produce those results? If courses are being delivered in ways that are out of alignment with the way that significant portions of the audience think and learn, companies are wasting tremendous amounts of money. Either the courses or the students generally get the blame: The courses weren't well designed and executed, or the students didn't apply themselves. But maybe the blame resides in the mismatch between delivery vehicle and learning style.

If you hope to maximize the results of top-down directives to support business strategies and produce a measurable impact on operations and revenue, an awareness of employees' learning styles is key.

From the other side—from a bottom-up perspective—questions about the efficient use of resources and the business impact of training can help learning professionals apply learning styles theory in reasonable ways. No organization can promise to give every employee learning experiences targeted specifically to his or her styles, any more than an honest elementary school educator can promise that every student's unique needs and gifts will be recognized, and that personalized instruction will be provided 100 percent of the time. We live in an imperfect world, and that's that. Yet there are things than can be done to design learning experiences in today's enterprises that make reasonable accommodations for learning styles research while also meeting the demands of senior management for cost containment and measurable business impact.

Determining the Dominant Styles of a Critical Workforce

One of the ways that enterprise learning can be delivered with a better return-on-investment is through focusing on so-called "business-critical" or "mission-critical" workforces. Tom Davenport and I conducted research recently on behalf of Accenture that underscores this fact. Rather than invest at equal levels in all employees, many organizations are focusing their training investments on workforces on the critical path to delivering business impact—in sales, customer service, or R&D—depending on the organization's particular industry and marketplace (Accenture 2007).

The next step companies might take from there would be to determine the dominant thinking and learning styles of that workforce. Research conducted by two Western Michigan professors, Charlotte Wenham and Raymond Alie, showed that learning-style differences do exist among occupations (Wenham & Alie 1992). Testing a variety of occupations, including technicians, secretaries, mechanical engineers, drafters/designers, and systems analysts, the researchers uncovered significant differences in preferred styles—differences that crossed gender and age categories. Other research has found correlations between a person's area of academic concentration at university and learning style preferences (see figure 8-3).

Such findings could help companies develop courses that are more aligned with the dominant learning styles of a particular kind of workforce. Companies might find, for example, that their salesforce is made up of people whose thinking and learning styles are, for example, intuitive, kinesthetic, and concrete-reflective. Learning experiences could then be designed to accommodate some critical subset of those styles, improving the impact of training on sales performance.

This is an excellent example of the top-down/bottom-up approach in action. From a top-down perspective, management mandates a focus on particular workforces to execute new strategies. From a bottom-up perspective, a focus on the appropriate learning styles for that workforce helps deliver a better return-on-investment, by improving the impact of training on the knowledge, skills, and behaviors of that workforce.

Figure 8-3. People's Learning Style Preferences Influence (and Are Influenced by) Their Choice of University Studies

Accommodators	Divergers
• Commerce • Education • Environmental Studies • Geography • Political Science • Public Policy	• English • History • Philosophy • Sociology
Convergers	**Assimilators**
• Applied Economics • Applied Physics • Art History • Computing • Engineering • Forestry • Law • Medical Research	• Astronomy • Chemistry • Classics • Earth Sciences • Economics • Mathematics • Theoretical Physics

Source: Adapted from "Learning cycles and learning styles: Kolb's experiential learning theory and its application in geography in higher education," by Mick Healey and Alan Jenkins. *Journal of Geography,* 99, pp. 185-195. Used with permission.

Making Varied Learning Experiences Available Through Technology

New learning technologies, especially consumer-driven technologies and trends such as MP3 players, blogs, and wikis, show promise of creating a situation I have called "learning for one" (Higgins & Mindrum 2007). Like packaged consumer food companies that sell individual servings (for instance, "soup for one"), enterprise learning appears to be evolving toward a similar kind of granularity and focus. "Learning for one" solutions would be flexible enough to be applied to broader workforces (especially focused, as noted, on their dominant learning styles), then more narrowly to specific roles, and then finally to individuals themselves.

The key here is to be aware of the powerful impact of learning styles on learning—not to be overwhelmed by the plethora of learning styles frameworks, but to pick vehicles that serve the needs of as many employees' styles as possible. For example, making a critical learning module available as text and as a downloadable podcast would go a long way toward accommodating individual needs. Extra costs?

Perhaps. But how does that cost compare to the waste of modules that have no discernible impact on many employees' performance?

The flexibility of e-learning and the increasing ability of learning management systems to provide multiple paths through the same content are also showing promise in being able to deliver learning experiences that are more aligned with an individual's preferred thinking and learning styles.

Two researchers from a technology institute in Ireland conducted an experiment where learners took an online course in three modules, each designed to appeal to a different learning style. (The experiment used a VAK model.) The experiment clearly showed that learners performed better on posttests for the modules designed for their dominant learning style (Brennan & McNutt 2004). Elsewhere, the authors of this study have termed this approach an "adaptive e-learning framework." For large organizations with dispersed workforces, where a focus on the dominant learning styles of a more or less unitary workforce is almost always impossible, adaptive learning solutions that accommodate multiple learning styles offer the promise of more than paying off the additional investment required.

Again, consider the top-down/bottom-up approach. Top-down mandates dictate certain kinds of content and experiences to be delivered through training. Yet it's the bottom-up analysis that helps choose the right technologies and the right design to optimize the experience for particular learners. The most frequently cited use of podcasting—downloading university lectures—leaves room for improvement. The fact that a noninteractive lecture from a college professor is also available as a downloadable MP3 file is unlikely to revolutionize either higher education or corporate learning.

In every technology field, there is an inevitable early phase where people feel obliged to take a "new wine in old skins" approach. The early use of filmmaking technology set up a static camera to record stage dramas; only gradually did pioneers use the technology to invent a new art form. Similarly, the early use of podcasting has been mostly to deliver old stuff in a different way.

But by applying the concept of learning styles, new technologies can be used more effectively to meet the needs of employee learners. Podcast-based learning will need to be designed and delivered as highly engaging bursts of training measured in two- to three-minute segments. This is especially true for those who are not natural auditory learners, but it is also more generally true. The average human attention span is not long enough to justify creating learning experiences using only long, unvaried podcasts.

Providing More Variety in Corporate Learning Approaches

The concept of thinking styles/learning styles puts a slightly different twist on the effort of instructional designers to provide variety in course design, especially instructor-led training. Thanks to the work of Kolb and others in experiential learning, corporate trainers are much more apt today to design courses that provide opportunities for learners to do more than passively absorb information. We know now that we have to provide, during a single learning course or experience, more active application of information that has been introduced in a more passive way—through a lecture or presentation. That application might be discussion, simulations, or other hands-on activities.

But the variety offered in a learning event does more than just reinforce knowledge for a particular learner; it also provides multiple opportunities for employees who learn in different ways to "get it." Those visual or kinesthetic or "random" learners who might not have gotten as much out of an introductory presentation have an opportunity to catch up during a discussion or an activity. Awareness of learning styles does not necessarily change the variety of experiences in an instructor-led class, but it certainly provides extra justification for the time and expense of designing with the multiple learning modalities of employees in mind.

Helping Employees Own More of Their Learning Responsibility

Finally, enterprise learning departments have an obligation to provide their employees with guided self-assessments that help them understand their thinking/learning styles and the implications of those styles for their jobs and their training experiences. A thinking styles/learning styles assessment needs to be a part of every organization's introductory training period for every employee. Numerous instruments are available for corporations wishing to perform assessments of their employees' thinking and learning styles. Some, like the Kolb Learning Styles Inventory, may involve a fee. A number of online assessments are free, though they are more limited and therefore of more limited value. But simply starting down the road, giving employees the means to better understand themselves and the distinctive ways they think and learn can enrich their jobs, their careers, and their contribution to the organization.

By helping employees understand their personal styles, we help them equip themselves to own more of their learning experience—something that will become increasingly important as specialization of jobs and roles increases, making it harder for learning departments to mass produce and deliver courses. Dan

Bielenberg, who heads up the strategy component for the internal training (capability development) team at Accenture, notes that his company is serving clients in ways that require employees to be increasingly specialized in their skills. That means that more employee-directed learning will be critical. The training organization will not be able to be everywhere it's needed. "As we look ahead," says Bielenberg, "we're pursuing the idea of 'roadmaps' for our people—guidance that helps them understand where they are, and what they need to do to progress to the next level of proficiency in a given subject area. Then, from a menu of options, they can choose the means to get there that is best for them—their experience, their motivation, and their learning styles."

That path, Bielenberg says, may take them through formal training or perhaps through collaboration and other kinds of informal learning experiences. "As training experts, we'll continue to deliver foundation training, and the offerings that might touch multiple workforces and thousands of people dispersed around the world—since there we want commonality as much as possible. But for many other employees, especially as they mature and specialize, we'll be providing guidance as much as anything. They will own more of their learning, based on their goals, their needs and their styles."

Know Thyself

"Know thyself" read the ancient inscription on the Temple of Apollo at Delphi. Self-knowledge (and even self-appreciation) sits at the heart of learning styles and thinking styles theory. Metacognition, or the awareness of our own mental processes, is critical for advancing our knowledge and skills. It is easy to despair at any age when fellow students or colleagues at work are "getting something" and we are not. But if we know who we are and what our styles are, we can cope. We can take steps to address a misalignment. We can even learn to improve our capabilities in a particular style.

There is untapped potential in so many of the employees who work with us and for us. By helping those employees understand their styles and their strengths, we can help them make a more significant contribution to the performance of the entire organization (see sidebar for more on planning a learning experience to accommodate different learning styles). That's the part of bottom-up learning design that resonates the loudest. We help our people—and our organizations—live up to what they are capable of becoming.

Planning a Learning Experience to Accommodate Different Learning Styles

Learning designers should incorporate as much variety of material and technique into a course as possible to appeal to different learning styles. This book is, of course, something that would appeal to visual/verbal learners. Here are examples of other mechanisms and techniques that would appeal to other types of learners.

Visual/Nonverbal

A video or chart makes information come alive for visual/nonverbal learners. These pie charts, for example, show the results from one study exploring gender differences in learning styles. The charts show the percentage of each gender that demonstrated visual (V), auditory (A), read/write (R), or kinesthetic (K) as their single-mode preferred learning style. It also shows those who were multi-modal. This information could easily be presented in bullet-point format, but this visual representation will be more easily assimilated by visual/nonverbal learners.

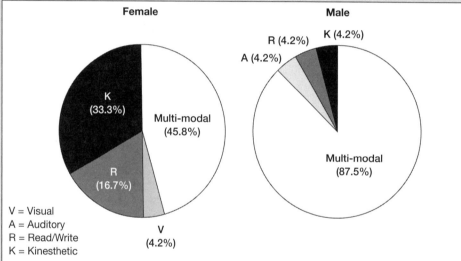

Source: Erica A. Wehrwein, Heidi L. Lujan and Stephen E. DiCarlo, "Gender differences in learning style preferences among undergraduate physiology students," *Advances in Physiological Education,* 31: 153-157, 2007. Copyright © 2007 American Physiological Society. Used with permission. Note: Percentages may not add to 100% due to rounding.

Auditory/Verbal

Discussion groups reinforce points made during passive, reading-based, and listening-based learning. Auditory/verbal learners benefit from a combination of listening and speaking. Here is an example of an assignment that would appeal to an auditory/verbal learner.

Course: Advanced sales techniques
Assignment: Small-group work
In groups of three or four, each person should tell the stories of both their best and their worst sales experiences, and then discuss within the group. For negative experiences, when did things begin to go wrong? What would you say were the causes of the bad

experience? If you could do things over, what would you do differently? Were there tools or job aids that you feel could have helped to make the experience successful?

For your best experiences, reflect on what felt right about how things went. Other than making a successful sale at the end, how could you tell things were going well? What general lessons can you take away from that experience?

Tactile/Kinesthetic

This type of learner benefits from experiential, hands-on application of principles or field work. Here is an assignment that might energize a tactile/kinesthetic learner.

Course: Delivering an effective customer experience through cross-selling and up-selling **Assignment:** Call your wireless phone provider to inquire into a charge that appeared on your bill last month. At the conclusion of the inquiry, did the service representative ask you if you would like to hear about other offers from the company? How effectively did the rep introduce the sales opportunity? Describe the experience from your point of view as a customer. If you felt the rep did an effective job, explain why. Likewise, if you reacted negatively to the sales pitch, tell why you felt that way.

■ ■ ■

Leveraging the Learning Advantage

■ Humans all have different thinking styles or cognitive styles and, hence, different learning styles.

■ The concepts of thinking styles and learning styles provide the business context for maximizing the effect of learning on workforce performance and the learning context that helps one apply new learning technologies.

■ Effective learning strategies are designed from the top down and the bottom up. They are informed by corporate strategy, but also by knowing how individuals learn most effectively.

■ Thinking styles are teachable, though certain kinds of jobs and roles may never be suited to a person's particular thinking or learning style. Organizations must have ways to identify such mismatches.

■ By applying the concept of learning styles, new technologies can be used more effectively to meet the needs of employee learners.

■ Learning professionals can analyze the dominant learning styles of particular roles or workforces, leading to the design of more effective training experiences.

■ The variety of activities and formats offered in a learning event does more than just reinforce knowledge for a particular learner; it also provides multiple opportunities for employees who learn in different ways to "get it."

■ By helping employees understand their own learning styles, enterprise learning departments help to equip them to own more of their training experience.

9

The Future of Learning and Human Resources

Susan Meisinger,
Former President and Chief Executive Officer
of SHRM (Society for Human Resource Management)

Executive Summary

The world is changing, and HR must change with it. In the face of challenges such as new technologies and globalization, HR professionals must take on new roles and continue to find innovative ways to deliver training.

In addition, the demand for new talent has never been greater. If HR cannot obtain the talent from outside of the organization, it must find a way to grow it from within. HR must also address the need for broader skills, with an emphasis on creativity and a return to basic qualities in workers—such as a solid work ethic—which are increasingly lacking in high school graduates.

Only by acquiring and using the HR competencies can HR and training professionals prepare themselves for the future.

Palmisano's Confidence

When Sam Palmisano, chief executive officer of IBM, announced his signature Business Transformation initiative, he established an on-demand global supply chain that provides customers with IBM products and services wherever and whenever they need them. He eliminated layers of management bureaucracy and moved the workforce closer to its global clients so the company could compete on service delivery.

Today, the information technology (IT) giant generates more than $90 billion in revenues. With 330,000 employees, it is among the 15 largest publicly traded companies in the world.

What made Palmisano think these bold changes were possible? The strength of his company's workforce and confidence in his HR team, for one. Palmisano knew his HR executives had the vision, skills, and drive required to develop and deploy a workforce strategy that would support the company's new way of doing business.

On Center Stage

HR's place in IBM's business plan is where HR is finding itself at many organizations—on center stage. Not fighting for a seat at the table. Not struggling to convince line executives that HR should be their business partner. Not feeling forced to defend the value HR adds.

At these organizations, expectations for HR are high. They are counting on HR to establish a ready supply chain of talent—from the executive suite to the factory floor—that will outperform the competition. At IBM, Palmisano has made it clear that if the company loses revenue or market share, HR will share in the blame (SHRM 2007a).

Still Room for Improvement

Despite progressive thinking at IBM and many other organizations, HR professionals still can face an uphill battle. In 2004, the Society for Human Resource Management (SHRM) asked CEOs, CFOs, chief human resource officers, and other executives at *Fortune* 1000 and mid-sized companies for their opinions on human capital. While the group universally said employees are critical assets, it also gave HR low marks on business and strategic leadership, the ability to get things done, innovation, and vision.

HR professionals need to take this feedback to heart. No one doubts HR professionals' knowledge of HR. But some executives continue to question HR's ability to perform at the highest levels.

New Expectations of HR

Many of these misgivings stem from the mismatch between old HR skills and new business realities. The world is changing in ways that put HR in the spotlight. There are many societal, demographic, economic, and political changes shaping the modern marketplace. A few key changes rise to the top. For example, as the demographics of the United States change, so do the demographics of potential recruits, current employees, and the young people who will make up tomorrow's workforce. Technology is changing the way organizations operate, serve customers, and develop new products and services. It's also dramatically changing the way HR is organized and delivered, as well as the expectations of return-on-investment for that technology.

In today's marketplace, globalization is bringing significant opportunities and questions for all organizations—and not just for multinational companies. Just as organizations compete globally for products and customers, so they must also compete for talent. HR is developing strategies to ensure competitiveness, not just in the talent pool, but in core business and workforce structures. Beating the competition means HR must be flexible and able to anticipate and master change.

All of these trends affect the expectations that executive management, boards of directors, and investors have for HR. The bottom line, as David Ulrich, a lead author of the *2007 HR Competency Study* (HRCS), puts it, is that "legacy HR work is going, and HR people who don't change with it will be gone" (SHRM 2007b).

The HR professionals who do make it will be the ones who embrace the new roles and competencies their organizations need. Conducted under the auspices of the Ross School of Business at the University of Michigan and The RBL Group in Salt Lake City, with regional partners that include SHRM in North America and other institutions in Latin America, Europe, China, and Australia, the HRCS defines those roles and competencies. Reflecting the continuing evolution of the HR profession, the six core competencies identified in the study supersede the five competencies outlined in the previous HRCS, released in 2002.

Three-Tier Pyramid of HR Competencies

To understand HR's six critical roles/competencies, it's helpful to view them as a three-tier pyramid with the most important—Credible Activist—at the top. *Credible Activists* are respected, admired, listened to, and offer a point of view. They take a position and challenge assumptions. They add value by delivering results with integrity, sharing information, building relationships of trust, and "doing HR with an attitude." This means taking appropriate risks, providing candid observations, and influencing others.

One level below Credible Activists, the second tier represents Cultural Stewards, Talent Managers/Organizational Designers, and Strategy Architects. *Cultural Stewards* recognize, articulate, and help shape their organizations' cultures by facilitating change, crafting culture, and turning knowledge into action. *Talent Managers/ Organizational Designers* focus on how talent enters, moves up, across, or out of the organization, and on the processes that shape how the organization works. Their linking reflects Ulrich's belief that HR may be placing too much emphasis on talent acquisition at the expense of organizational design. Talent management will not succeed in the long run without an organizational structure that supports it. And, finally, *Strategy Architects* require a vision of how the organization can succeed in the future, and demand an active part in establishing overall strategy to deliver that vision. They recognize business trends and their impact on the business, and identify potential roadblocks and opportunities.

Except in China, where HR is at an earlier stage in professional development and there is great emphasis on transactional activities, the final two competencies representatives in the third tier—Business Allies and Operational Executors—are looked upon as basic skills that everyone must have. *Business Allies* know the environment their organizations operate in, how they make money, who their customers are, and why they buy their products and services. They also understand the basics of functions such as finance and marketing. *Operational Executors* ensure the basics are covered. They create, adapt, and implement policies that efficiently deliver compensation, benefits, relocations, performance management, and other essential HR functions. One danger for HR is giving this competency short shrift while focusing on others; Ulrich warns there's risk in paying too little attention to these nuts-and-bolts activities.

While excelling in all six competency areas sounds daunting, HR professionals who want to be key contributors to the success of their organizations will embrace the challenge. To start, Ulrich recommends HR professionals initiate three conversations. The first should be with business leaders to review the competencies and compare their own skills against theirs. The second should be with their HR teams to get their perspectives. And the third should be with themselves. Once gaps are identified, they can set priorities to develop their knowledge and skills (SHRM 2007b).

Where and How Learning Fits In

These competencies will be sorely needed over the next several years by both HR professionals and those tasked with learning responsibilities outside of HR. No matter what an organization's goals are—rapid expansion, new products, or simply "business as usual"—one of the most important questions HR professionals will need to ask is, "Do we have the talent we need to carry out our objectives?" If the answer is no—and often it will be—they'll need to put all of their competencies and knowledge to work to get that talent on board. They will need to address the talent question early in the organizational strategy process and be able to identify and then fill the gaps in the workforce, either by finding new talent or building it from within.

Raise Questions from the Outset

HR professionals and, if there are separate learning or training functions, their partners from those areas, need to start answering the talent question *before* the organizational strategy is decided. By performing and sharing due diligence during strategy development, HR professionals help their organizations make better choices by identifying people issues that could make or break a particular initiative.

Consider a company that wants to expand into Europe or Asia. This scenario is increasingly common; companies around the world are finding that growth requires expansion into international markets. Nearly three out of five (58 percent) participants in a 2006 Accenture survey said their most recent acquisition took place across national borders; more than one-quarter (26 percent) view cross-border acquisitions as necessary to survive (SHRM 2007c).

While such expansion may bring growth, it also poses significant HR challenges. Some key workforce development issues to be considered include the existing skill level of the target country's workforce, the availability of managerial talent who are able to bridge both cultures, and the training timelines and costs associated with staffing the new entity. The educational needs of employees in other locations who will interact with the new entity also must be weighed.

Address the Talent Gap: Find It or Build It

The question, "Do we have enough talent?" needs to be asked again once organizational goals have been set. It's up to HR to develop, sell, and deploy a workforce plan that puts the right people in the right place now and creates a pipeline to replace them should their availability or company needs and priorities change.

Fortunately, technology and new data-mining capabilities make it much easier for organizations today to keep track of who in their organizations has which skills and competencies and where he or she is currently positioned. Data analysis also can reveal the skills that might soon be lost to retirements or other demographic changes. And, by reviewing external market data, HR can get a strong sense of the competition for individuals with certain skills or knowledge.

Once the gaps between future needs and present capabilities are identified, HR has two options for getting the talent it needs: hire it externally or build it internally. With talent markets expected to be tight in the coming years, especially for the best and brightest employees, the latter will be increasingly important. Giving current workers the skills they need to contribute to organizational goals reduces the organization's need to compete for talent in a crowded marketplace.

Types of Development

Some of the most important learning that HR and the learning function will need to deliver isn't tied to specific skills, such as knowing a particular software program or accounting system. While training associated with those areas has its place, organizations have a critical need for broader skills that will help employees succeed, no matter what their roles or organizational goals—skills including creativity/innovation, leadership, cross-cultural expertise, and basic workplace skills.

Creativity and Innovation

As technology absorbs many jobs once done by people, creativity and innovative thinking are increasingly regarded as an important source of not only competitive advantage but also future jobs. Along with automation, the offshoring of routine work is leading many business forecasters to predict that the majority of jobs remaining in developed countries like the United States will emphasize a new set of skills.

Although the ability to think logically and analytically will remain important, experts predict organizations will also place greater importance on right-brained capabilities such as "big picture" thinking and the ability to bring together disparate ideas to create new synergies, products, and services (Workplace Visions 2007). Nearly three-quarters (74 percent) of participants in a collaborative study from the Conference Board, Corporate Voices for Working Families, the Partnership for 21st Century Skills, and SHRM expect demand for these skills to increase in importance over the next five years (Conference Board et al. 2006).

Given this reality, HR clearly must consider strategies to improve the creative environment of the workforce both now and in the future. Fittingly, this will require creativity and innovation on the part of HR itself.

Leadership Development

Another important area will be leadership development. With the impending retirement of the baby-boom generation, changing demographics, and limited resources, leadership development is rising to the top as an organizational priority. At the same time, a new paradigm is emerging, shifting from authoritative leadership and position power to collaborative leadership and knowledge power.

Three-quarters (74 percent) of participants in the SHRM 2006 HR Strategic Management Survey perceive leadership development as one of the core areas where HR can make a strategic contribution. Examples of steps HR can take to improve leadership skills include the following (Lockwood 2005):

- Assessing leadership styles and motives and determining their impact on climate and performance
- Creating customized, competency-driven leadership models to support the organization's strategic goals
- Focusing on and expanding the emotional intelligence of their leadership (namely, self-awareness, self-management, social awareness, and social skills)
- Demonstrating a strong commitment to extensive development and coaching efforts
- Measuring and rewarding both leadership development and performance.

Learning options for leadership development shown to be successful include 360-degree feedback, assessment instruments, formal or informal mentoring, executive coaching, on-the-job experience (such as rotational assignments and action learning), off-the-job experience (such as community leadership and industry associations), and leadership scorecards (Lockwood 2005).

An important area for HR professionals to consider when focusing on leadership development is diversity in the pipeline. Research shows that organizations are not optimizing leadership development opportunities for diverse groups. Solutions include holding managers accountable for training on diversity and associated attitudes and behaviors, as well as making progress on diversity metrics (SHRM 2006a).

Cross-Cultural Skills

A third of the survey participants are in need of development is cross-cultural skills. According to the *SHRM 2006 Workplace Forecast*, a biannual summary of the trends expected to have the greatest impact on the workplace over the next decade, the number-one action that organizations are taking in response to international trends is to expand into the global marketplace. While the need to develop cross-cultural skills within international organizations is obvious, even organizations with no plans to move into the global market need to cultivate cross-cultural expertise within their ranks. Cultural issues may play crucial roles in decisions to offshore, working through supply chains, and recruiting needed foreign talent, for example.

In addition, while English has established itself as the world's business language, a more culturally diverse global business environment means that a multitude of languages may be spoken, depending on the context. This shift could lead to increased expectations of language skills among executives and greater investment in language training (SHRM 2006b).

Skills related to ethics and social responsibility also are increasingly in demand. The ability to balance ethics and financial considerations is especially important, as are competencies related to promoting social responsibility both within and outside the organization.

Back to Basics

Finally, basic skills can't be overlooked. A survey conducted in 2006 by the Conference Board, Corporate Voices for Working Families, the Partnership for 21st Century Skills, and SHRM found that the generation coming into the workplace sorely lacks both basic academic and more advanced "applied" skills (Conference Board et al. 2006).

Employers expect young people to arrive with a core set of basic knowledge and the ability to apply their skills in the workplace, but the reality is not matching their expectations. Seven out of 10 survey participants cited deficiencies among incoming high school graduates in "applied" skills, such as professionalism and work ethic, a category that includes skills such as personal accountability, punctuality, working productively with others, and time and workload management. Participants also said recent high school graduates lack basic skills in reading comprehension, writing, and math. More than eight out of 10 (81 percent) said high school graduates were deficient in written communications, for example (Conference Board et al. 2006).

A study conducted by the U.S. Department of Education and Institute of Education Sciences suggests the problem won't disappear anytime soon. The 2005 National Assessment of Educational Progress found that only 35 percent of 12th graders were "proficient" or better in reading. For math, the numbers were even worse; less than one-quarter (23 percent) ranked as proficient or better. Nearly two out of five (39 percent) lacked even rudimentary skills (NAEP 2006).

HR professionals need to address the basic skills problem on two levels:

- First, they must put workplace programs and initiatives in place to develop these skills in employees while on the job.
- Second, they must also work within their local communities to focus educators and students on required skills for future jobs.

Meeting Employee Expectations

To develop employees in these and other areas, HR and the learning function will have to work in tandem, no matter what the reporting relationship. Programs and initiatives will need to be developed that take into account the realities and expectations of today's workforce. Take the evolution and revolution of technology. Just a few years ago, most learning was delivered in person; today the Internet, wireless technologies, portable devices, and other innovations are allowing organizations to deliver learning through multiple channels.

That's exactly what's needed to reach younger, tech-savvy workers, according to SkillSoft, a provider of e-learning and performance support solutions. The company notes that the learning styles and habits of the latest generation to enter the workplace have been strongly affected by their vast experience using technology; their constant bombardment by rich, multimedia content; and the seemingly effortless way in which they multitask while using a diverse range of digital media. To leverage this, SkillSoft recommends that employers provide such workers with these types of learning experiences:

- **Multiple-media driven.** Because this generation grew up with televisions, computers, video games, DVDs, and personal music devices, their brains are wired to receive visual and audio stimulation, often coming from multiple sources simultaneously. Raised on the sophisticated programming techniques of television and video games, they have high expectations for all forms of communication and demand highly produced, entertaining experiences. While not all training can or should be created with entertainment value as a primary objective, it is a good practice to intersperse multimedia learning and training resources that incorporate graphics, audio, and video, in addition to standard text.

- **Interactive.** Recent graduates entering the workforce expect interactivity as part of their learning experiences, whether it takes place in the classroom or online. As a result, static PowerPoint presentations, packets of handouts, and lectures no longer are the best way to deliver information and learning. Companies that want to engage their young employees should supplement static training with simulations and other forms of learning that require active participation. Multi-path gaming techniques, for instance, put learners in control, enabling them to freely navigate a simulated workplace (complete with virtual colleagues, ringing telephones, and documents on the desktop) to analyze and solve business problems. Virtual classroom sessions can also be used to bring together groups of learners to interact and discuss topics that have been covered in online self-study.

- **On-Demand.** At their peak while multitasking, this generation doesn't have the interest or attention span to sit through an entire course from beginning to end. Instead, they prefer to learn by consuming small, digestible bits of information—a section of an e-learning course, a specific chapter within a reference work, or a two- to three-minute video. Organizations can cater to their comfort by making these various learning assets available on-demand. Supported by strong search functionality, employees can easily pinpoint exactly the information they need, precisely at the moment they need it.

- **Integrated.** While classroom training will always have a role in professional development, learning, for the most part, should not be a discrete event that removes employees from the workplace. Rather, organizations should bring learning to the learners, making it an inherent part of the workday that is easily accessible via the corporate intranet or portal. This affords employees the flexibility to pick and choose, cafeteria style, the exact combination of information resources they need for the work at hand, ensuring greater retention, productivity, and improved performance.

- **Mobile.** Constantly on the go, this generation relies on portable devices like cell phones, BlackBerry devices, and Treos to do everything from making phone calls and checking email to browsing the Internet and playing games. Organizations can take advantage of the growing ubiquity of portable devices to make learning assets that were traditionally only available at the office accessible to workers, regardless of their location, so that they can capitalize on downtime to develop new competencies or hone existing skills. In addition, podcasts provide another effective mechanism for learning on the go, as information on business issues, trends, and initiatives can be downloaded to laptops, iPods, and other MP3 players for quick, easy consumption.

At the same time, HR professionals will have to deliver training in ways that appeal to less tech-savvy, media-oriented employees. Employees used to high-touch, rather than high-tech, methods will continue to expect opportunities for personal interaction and instructor-led learning.

Time Management and Balance

Training and learning initiatives also will have to reflect employees' growing demand for greater work–life balance. Taking classes at community colleges, attending out-of-town conferences and workshops, or even taking time away from primary work responsibilities for training have little appeal to employees struggling to juggle childcare, eldercare, and other personal responsibilities.

The SHRM 2006 Workplace Forecast shows that employees born after 1965 are more likely to have multiple caring responsibilities that are more equally shared between the sexes, making demands for work–life balance an issue for both female and male employees. In addition, work–life balance seems to be a generational value for these employees, rather than a "life phase" issue, so it is likely to remain important through all phases of their career advancement.

Accessibility

Another expectation HR must be prepared for is training accessibility. This means providing experiences and materials that are appropriate for audiences who may have physical or cognitive disabilities or that have below-average comprehension of the primary language.

Take the case of employees with attention deficit/hyperactivity disorder (ADHD). A neurobiological disorder that affects more than 8 million adults in the United States, ADHD is usually characterized by impulsivity, inattention, and overactivity (Job Accommodation Network 2007). For employees with this condition, long, auditory-based training sessions may be impossible to process.

For employees more comfortable in a second language, multilingual resources should be considered, especially for education on critical issues. According to the U.S. Department of Labor, a disproportionate number of the accidents that happen involve Hispanic workers. The BEST Institute, a safety training firm specializing in cross-cultural issues, attributes the higher rate to language barriers, differences in learning styles, and cultural nuances. Even the best safety training is a poor prevention tool if it's presented in a language or manner that employees don't easily understand.

Making It Happen

Meeting employee expectations for learning is a moot point if HR doesn't have the resources available to offer it. That's where it pays to be steeped in HR's core competencies. The first step is making the business case for investment by tying learning initiatives to the organizational strategy. Getting buy-in from the top requires detailing not only the goals of the initiative, but how they will be achieved and—crucially—measured.

Randy MacDonald, senior vice president of HR at IBM, is one HR executive who gets this. To help the company achieve Palmisano's on-demand objective, MacDonald undertook a worldwide, $100 million reorganization of HR. To get the $100 million, he had to be a credible activist, strategy architect, cultural steward, and talent manager all at the same time to persuade the C suite that it was a good investment. "Do you think I can walk into the [office of the] CEO or CFO and ask for $100 million because I went to St. Francis College and I'm a good guy?" he says. "I told them, 'I'm going to deliver talent to you that's skilled and on time and ready to be deployed. I will be able to measure these skills, tell you what skills we have, what [skills] we don't have, [and] then show you how to fill the gaps or enhance our training'" (*Business Review* 2007).

Engaging Employees

Clear, frequent communication that explains the value of the offered learning experience to both the employee and the organization is important. Training expectations should be included in performance management plans, and employees should have input into the content and type of learning they receive.

Learning must be continuous. Research on employee orientations, for example, has shown that one month later, employees have lost much of the information provided to them (*Business Review* 2007). Important messages and skills must be regularly reinforced to be effective.

Sharing the Burden

To encourage buy-in and compliance with training initiatives, HR professionals should consider assigning accountability throughout the organization. That's what IBM did—95 percent of the $700 million it spent on training last year came out of line managers' budgets. Once the training line item appeared in managers' budgets, both HR and the line managers had compelling reasons to want the initiatives to succeed.

Measuring Outcomes

It's not enough for HR professionals to put systems, policies, and programs in place that they think will maximize human capital. They have to put systems, policies, and programs in place that they know will do the job. The only way to make that determination is to engage in continuous measurement.

There is an old saying that most people use statistics the way a drunk person uses a lamp post—more for support than for enlightenment. To add value, HR professionals must avoid falling into that trap. Measurement must be active, not passive, yielding information that can be turned into action. It also must be continuous. What point is there in measuring something just once and then walking away?

IBM's vice president of learning, Ted Hoff, says that developing training metrics is a difficult intellectual exercise, but worth the effort. "If you can figure out how to do them, they'll give you guidance about what's working and, equally important, they'll help you demonstrate your value. There are two challenges: 1) getting the goals clear and figuring out what metrics you can set against the goal, and 2) getting the data reasonably attainable and clean so you can do the measurements," says Hoff (SHRM 2007a).

The most reliable method is to have a participant group and a control group. But business units, eager to cash in on learning, usually aren't interested in holding one group back as a control. Hoff cites a case, however, where a controlled study helped him prove his value when training IBM client executives. The training was offered through the Internet. Some leaders encouraged their client execs to tap into it; some did not.

"We looked at the bottom-line performance of clusters of sales executives who took advantage of 15 online modules or more, versus the clusters of executives who, on average, took advantage of five or less. The results showed the executives who took 15 or more modules achieved a quota attainment of 107 percent over the quarter;

those in the cluster with five or less achieved a quota of 94 percent. The quota attainment difference was worth over $500 million in revenue. Gross margin was 30 percent. The e-learning investment was $12 million. That's $150 million in gross margin against a learning investment of $12 million," says Hoff (SHRM 2007a).

How the Workforce Development Staff Can Get Ready for the Future

Given all this, what do HR and learning professionals need to do to get ready for the future? The most important thing is to acquire and use the HR competencies and skills needed to contribute in the current business environment. Start by reviewing the HRCS competency model. Follow Ulrich's recommendation to seek feedback from senior executives and the HR team. In which of the competency areas do you excel? In which ones do you need work? What are the barriers preventing you from achieving success? Are they personal? Organizational? What support do you need to acquire these competencies?

It's also critical to develop HR competencies in others, and that means encouraging changes in HR education. Today, too much of academia provides knowledge for the HR jobs of the past rather than for the HR jobs of the future. Steps to providing better education include determining the core base of knowledge to be offered, improving the linkage between academics and practitioners, and improving the availability of internship programs that provide students with real-world perspectives (SHRM 2004).

HR and learning professionals also need to hone their collaboration skills to successfully manage internal and external relationships. While learning has always involved partnerships with external providers, the explosion of new technologies has greatly increased the number and types of third-party resources. Strong collaborative skills will be needed to select, manage, and measure the effectiveness of external partners.

The Bottom Line

The HR profession has made enormous strides over the past decade, but HR and learning professionals have no time to sit back and rest on their laurels. With changes in the business environment requiring new skills and new strategies, they need to get on board if they want to continue to make progress. Jean Halloran, senior vice president at Agilent Technologies Inc., says it best: "People talk about strategic HR, a place at the table, next to the CEO. I could have a place at the table and be irrelevant. Every step of the way I should be concerned if I am adding to the value of the business" (SHRM 2007d).

To that end, HR and learning professionals need to focus on several key action items:

- Assess personal competencies against those identified in the Human Resource Competency Study.
- Perform due diligence on human capital issues during the development phase of the organizational strategy.
- Undertake workforce audits to identify skills gaps based on current and projected business objectives.
- Develop workforce development strategies that clearly support organizational goals and incorporate the learning expectations and needs of a diverse workforce.
- Use strong metrics to measure the impact of training and education initiatives.

■ ■ ■

Leveraging the Learning Advantage

- Societal, demographic, economic, and political changes and their effects on the workforce are putting HR in the spotlight as never before.
- HR professionals today must master the six HR roles and competencies: Credible Activists, Cultural Stewards, Talent Managers/Organizational Designers, Strategy Architects, Business Allies, and Operational Executors.
- Confronting the challenge of finding new talent for an organization, HR has two choices: hire it or build it.
- Creative, innovative, right-brained thinking is growing in importance in today's workforce, as are leadership development, cross-cultural skills, and applied skills.
- Today's learning should be delivered through multiple channels, reflect employees' increasing demand for work–life balance, and be accessible.
- Buy-in for training can be secured by tying learning to the strategy of the organization.

10

Creating Value for Your Organization — The Way Forward

Karen Mantyla

Perhaps you're successfully holding on to your training dollars and have not had to deal with major cuts to your training budget. Perhaps you have been struggling to keep your training budget intact, forced to do more with less. Or perhaps your situation lies somewhere between these two opposites. Wherever you find yourself in today's challenging business environment, it is clear that in your role as a learning professional, your training content and applications must create proven and ongoing value for your organization. The ideas and concepts in this book can help you and others on your team take the next steps toward successfully aligning learning with strategy and technology.

Leverage the Lessons of the Case Studies

The contributing authors are leading experts in their fields. They have presented the lessons they have learned in implementing a blend of technology, learning, and strategy in their own organizations—sharing ideas, problems, opportunities, what worked and what didn't work, and why. They have also documented the value these programs have added to their organizations. Think of the case studies as listening to someone at a conference break-out session or at a local meeting. Use the key points in the Leveraging the Learning Advantage sections summarized at the end of each chapter as a map to help you negotiate the challenging road ahead for learning professionals and their organizations. Consider focusing on an area that will have the greatest impact for your organization. Take it a step at a time, and determine the right steps for you and your organization.

Create Value—and Be Able to Communicate That Value

Once you align your learning efforts to bottom-line metrics, your case for learning initiatives becomes stronger. If you are viewed as a strategic enhancer, your value to your organization increases. At given intervals, monitor the pulse of what value means for your decision makers. Their priorities represent a moving target. Keep your plan current, vital, and reflective of what value means *today*. At a time when business skills are more important than ever, show yourself to be an agile, flexible, and vital 21st century workforce development professional who understands business and the need to provide value to the bottom line.

Use Technology to Support Learning

Think about what options and opportunities exist to leverage technology to achieve learning outcomes. The great thing about technology is that each method of distribution can be used for so many different purposes. Take webinars, for example. How many different ways can you brainstorm to use webinars to target strategic learning events and outcomes? Instead of allowing the myriad technology choices to become overwhelming, isolate each technology available, and review it to see how it might support your strategic plan. Then, watch your ideas flow.

Plan for Success

The constant barrage of technology applications and solutions coming at us can seem mind-boggling. You may find it helpful to keep a planning document at your fingertips, in which you can capture information and ideas and track possible learning applications for your employees, customers, and partners. A planning document can help you organize your thoughts so that you can ask the experts the right questions. With that as your starting point, you can then identify the elements that support your strategic and workforce development plans. It's a powerful and simple way to chunk a lot of information at one time, and over time you will develop your own template to identify technology options that will support your success.

■ ■ ■

Your goal is to keep your training budget intact because you understand that learning can provide a true competitive advantage to your organization. When that happens and you find yourself holding on to training dollars that might have otherwise been lost in budget cuts, this book will have served its purpose.

■ ■ ■ References

Accenture. 2007. "Driving High Performance through Mission-Critical Job Families." www.accenture.com/Global/Outsourcing/Business_Process_Outsourcing/Accenture_ Learning/R_and_I/DrivingFamilies.htm.

Balaguer, Ellen, John G. Higgins, and Craig Mindrum. 2006. Connecting the Dots: Linking Enterprise Learning to High Performance. Available on Accenture site: www. accenture.com.

Barksdale, Susan, and Teri Lund. 2006. *10 Steps to Successful Strategic Planning*. Alexandria, VA: ASTD Press.

Brennan, Marie, and Larry McNutt. 2004. "An Adaptive eLearning Framework: Design Issues and Considerations." *ITB Journal*, no. 9, May.

———. 2006. "Learning Styles and Learning to Program: An Experiment in Adapting Online Resources to Match a Student's Learning Style." In *Proceedings of the International Conference on Innovation, Good Practice, and Research in Engineering Education*, ed. Susan Doyle and Adam Mannis. Available at http://www.ee2006.info/ presentations.html#Monday.

Business Review. 2007. "Measuring the Effects of Employee Orientation Training on Employee Perceptions of Vision and Leadership: Implications for Human Resources." *Business Review*, Summer.

Coffield, F., D. Moseley, E. Hall, and K. Ecclestone. 2004. *Learning Styles and Pedagogy in Post-16 Learning: A Systematic and Critical Review.* London: Learning and Skills Research Centre.

Conference Board, Corporate Voices for Working Families, Partnership for 21st Century Skills, and SHRM. 2006. "Are They Really Ready to Work?" *Survey Report*. Alexandria, VA: SHRM.

Gardner, Howard. 1993. *Frames of Mind: The Theory of Multiple Intelligences.* New York: Basic Books.

Gregorc, Anthony F. 2006. *The Mind Styles Model: Theory, Principles, and Practice.* Columbia, CT: Gregorc Associates Inc.

Higgins, John G., and Craig Mindrum. 2007. "Learning for One." *HR Director*, May.

Job Accommodation Network. 2007. "Employees with Attention Deficit/Hyperactivity Disorder." Available http://www.jan.wvu.edu/media/adhd.html.

Jung, C.G. 1923. *Psychological Types.* New York: Harcourt Brace.

Knighton, Tom. 2007. "Global Business Leaders Call for 'Speed Competence' 2008." *HR Trend Book.* Alexandria, VA: Society of Human Resource Management. Available at http://moss07.shrm.org/publications/hrmagazine/editorialcontent/pages/1207TRENDtraining.aspx.

Levine, Mel. 2003. *A Mind at a Time.* New York: Simon and Schuster.

Lockwood, Nancy. 2005. "Leadership Development" in SHRM Research, Briefly Noted, July. Available http://tinyurl.com/26c6xx.

Mantyla, Karen. 2001. *Blending E-Learning: The Power Is in the Mix.* Alexandria, VA: ASTD, 2001.

Metcalf, David S., II. 2006. *mLearning: Mobile Learning and Performance in the Palm of Your Hand.* Amherst, MA: HRD Press.

NAEP (National Assessment of Educational Progress). 2006. *The Nation's Report Card™.* NCES no. 2006-451. Washington, DC: U.S. Department of Education and Institute of Educational Sciences.

Riding, Richard, and Stephen Rayner. 1998. *Cognitive Styles and Learning Strategies: Understanding Style Differences in Learning and Behavior.* London: David Fulton Publishers.

Rivera, Ray. 2007. *WLP Scorecard: Why Learning Matters.* Alexandria, VA: ASTD Press.

Schramm, Jennifer. 2007. *Workplace Visions.* No.1. Alexandria, VA: SHRM.

SHRM. 2004. *Symposium on the Future of HR Education.* December.

———. 2006a. "Leadership Development: Optimizing Human Capital for Business Success." *SHRM Research Quarterly.*

———. 2006b. *SHRM 2006 Workplace Forecast.* Alexandria, VA: SHRM.

———. 2007a. "IBM's HR Takes a Risk." *HRMagazine,* June.

———. 2007b. "New Competencies for HR." *HRMagazine,* June.

———. 2007c. "Show All Employees a Wider World," *HRMagazine,* June.

———. 2007d. "HR at The Summit." *HRMagazine,* July.

Sternberg, Robert. 1997. *Thinking Styles.* New York: Cambridge University Press.

Vanthournout, Donald. 2006. *Return on Learning: Training for High Performance at Accenture.* Evanston, IL: Agate.

Wenham, Charlotte, and Raymond E. Alie. 1992. "Learning Styles and Corporate Training." *American Journal of Business,* 7(1): 3-10.

■■■ About the Editor and Contributors

Karen Mantyla, CDE, is President of Quiet Power, Inc., a Washington, D.C.-based distance learning training and consulting company (www.quietpower.com). Mantyla has over 25 years of specialized experience in the development and implementation of workplace education programs, with specific emphasis on reaching learners in dispersed geographic locations. She held many senior leadership positions, including vice president of a *Fortune* 500 company. She also provides executive and supervisory coaching services focusing on helping clients learn and strengthen effective leadership skills. An executive coach since 1996, she utilizes various technology distribution methods to support the needs of her clients.

She consults with both public and private sector clients to help design, develop, implement, and maintain learner-centered distance learning programs. Her focus is on the "human side" of the distance learning equation to ensure that senior management, human resource personnel, and learners receive proper support, guidance, and training for success in their distance learning initiatives and programs. In addition, she helps design learner support systems, tools, and methods to ensure success and continuous process improvement for remote site facilitators, coaches, and learners.

She is the author of many best-selling books, including *Blending E-Learning: The Power Is in the Mix* (ASTD 2001); *Interactive Distance Learning Exercises That Really Work!* (ASTD 1999); lead author of *Distance Learning: A Step-By-Step Guide for Trainers* (ASTD 1997); editor of *The 2000/2001 ASTD Distance Learning Yearbook* (McGraw-Hill 2000); coeditor of *The 2001/2002 ASTD Distance Learning Yearbook* (McGraw-Hill 2001) and *Consultative Sales Power* (Crisp Publications 1995).

Mantyla is an active member of the American Society for Training & Development (ASTD) and is often called upon to be an expert reviewer for the annual ASTD Excellence in Practice Awards. She has served on the board of directors and as secretary of the FGDLA (Federal Government Distance Learning Association), where she was also editor of *Distance Learning News,* the official publication of FGDLA. She was nominated and elected to the FGDLA Hall of Fame in 2003 for advancing the field of distance education in the federal government.

She received her professional certification in distance learning from the University of Wisconsin-Madison, a renowned leader in distance education.

Contributors

Michael Gerwitz, CDE, is project manager for the U.S. Department of Labor's e-learning initiative. He is responsible for implementing an enterprisewide e-learning solution consisting of learning and content management systems. He also serves as the director of e-learning for the U.S. Occupational Safety and Health Administration. In this capacity, he employed open-source software to develop a government-owned web publishing application. Gerwitz served as the director of distance learning for the Department of Defense's Defense Logistics Agency for seven years. He has 15 years of experience using technology-based solutions to enhance the performance and productivity of individuals. He is a key liaison between government and the commercial sector and continues to lead technical efforts that promote the portability and interoperability of systems and applications government and industrywide. He earned his professional certification from the University of Wisconsin.

Frederick Goh, at the time of the writing of this volume, was the director of Strategic Learning at Caterpillar University. As chief learning strategist, he had responsibility for enterprise learning strategy, benchmarking, and best practices within the learning and development space. In 2000, Goh was a member of the strategy team that recommended the creation of Caterpillar University to institutionalize Continual Learning, and in 2001 he was appointed as its first dean. He also directed the development and deployment of Caterpillar's Enterprise Learning Plan framework. Over the past year, his work has focused on the impact of learning and development on employee engagement to take Caterpillar's learning strategy to the next level. Goh's 26-year career spans the fields of engineering, marketing, management consulting, strategic business planning, and human resources. He holds a BBA degree from Royal Melbourne Institute of Technology

University in Australia and an MS in Human Resource Development from South Bank University, United Kingdom.

Michael Hatt, director of training for American Express Learning Network, Phoenix, has over 11 years in the instructional design, development, and delivery fields. Having worked with Computer Sciences Corporation, Bank of America, Microsoft, and now American Express, he has led teams large and small to build and deploy innovative training solutions for both internal and external business partners. His practical application of training covers several core business functions including technical troubleshooting, customer service skills, as well as sales and retention skills that provide support to many of his innovative training ideas. These diverse experiences have helped prove that his workflow-based training models and re-usable learning objects strategies save companies untold sums of money through re-use and strategic alignment of training direction. He specializes in using adult learning theory with an innovative practical application approach to solve business problems on a global scale. Hatt was responsible for training the ever-growing Xbox support business and for taking American Express training to the next level in its Phoenix location. He has presented to audiences in Argentina, Canada, Egypt, Estonia, Germany, Philippines, and the United States. He presented his best-in-class solution at the Microsoft Learning Conference in 2007 discussing adult learning theories and using advanced technologies to solve training-related issues as part of blended training solutions. In 2008 he won the inaugural Learning Innovation award at Microsoft for innovation in using technology in training.

Michael Malehorn is an experienced project manager with over 15 years of experience in the analysis, design, and development of Internet-based software with a focus on e-learning projects and applications. This experience includes direct experience in requirements generation/needs analysis, acquisition and procurement, and implementation strategies for e-learning programs and systems in support of government and corporate clients. Malehorn currently leads SI International Inc.'s E-Learning Infrastructure business practice as one of the company's senior managers. In this capacity, he provides consulting services to government clients in the areas of requirements generation, acquisition planning, and implementation and integration support for e-learning solutions in clients' technical architecture and training environments. His focus over the past five years has been in assisting federal government clients in the identification, implementation, and integration of learning management and learning content management systems.

Susan Meisinger, SPHR, JD, is retired president and chief executive officer of the Society for Human Resource Management (SHRM), the world's largest professional association devoted to human resource management. Under her leadership, SHRM grew from 170,000 members to more than 245,000, and was recognized as one of the top 50 "Great Places to Work" in the Washington, D.C., area. Prior to joining the society, Meisinger served as deputy undersecretary in the U.S. Department of Labor. Meisinger has extensive experience in board governance. In the nonprofit sector, from 2004 to 2008, she served as a board member for the World Federation of Personnel Management Associations, a global federation of associations, and served as secretary-general from 2006 to 2008. She sat on both the SHRM board and Human Resource Certification Institute board, and served on the board of the Ethics Resource Center from 2000 to 2008. Meisinger also has experience in the for-profit sector, having sat on the board for BE&K, a multibillion-dollar international design-build firm, also serving on the audit and compensation committees. Meisinger received a bachelor's degree from Mary Washington College and a law degree from the National Law Center of George Washington University. She is certified as a senior professional in human resources.

Craig Mindrum, PhD, is a strategic and talent management consultant who describes his own preferred learning style as "visual-verbal-reading-random-dialogic-chaotic." Over a 27-year career as a businessman, researcher, author, and a college professor at DePaul and Indiana universities, he has focused on areas of human performance and organizational change, including learning, communications, leadership, and the moral design of organizations. He has coauthored several books, including *Return on Learning* (Agate 2006) and *FutureWork: Putting Knowledge to Work in the Knowledge Economy* (Free Press 1997). He has written numerous articles and book chapters, including "Human Performance that Increases Business Performance" in *Breaking the Code of Change* (Harvard Business School Press 2000). Following master's degree studies at Yale University and Indiana University, Mindrum received his doctorate from the University of Chicago. He lives in Oak Park, Illinois, near Chicago, with his wife, Donna, and his three children, Jonathan, Jennifer, and Jessica.

Kurt Olson, PhD, as director of capability solutions for Accenture, oversees the curriculum planning activities for Accenture's employees worldwide. Olson has spent most of his 23-year career with Accenture working in the learning industry. His passion for his work comes from the opportunity to directly and positively impact every employee of Accenture and, in turn, to positively impact Accenture's clients. Olson has a patent pending on the "phenomenal learning" methodology that Accenture developed to support its learning design and development process. He earned a BS in computer science from Illinois State University and an MBA from Northern Illinois University. He recently earned a PhD in organization development from Benedictine University. In addition, he is a Six Sigma Black Belt. His inspiration comes from his wife, Shelly, and their sons, Michael and Connor.

Don Vanthournout, Accenture's chief learning officer, is in charge of the capability development needs, including learning and knowledge management, of the company's more than 180,000 employees located in 49 countries. After graduating from Bradley University in 1981 with a BS in mathematics and secondary education, with a business minor, Vanthournout joined Accenture and spent almost 15 years working with external clients before moving into a series of director-level roles in the company's learning organization. In 2001, he became the head of Accenture's Capability Development organization and was subsequently named chief learning officer. Vanthournout is active in his church where his passion is working with high school students.

◼ ◼ ◼ Index

In this index, *f* represents a figure and *t* represents a table.